Beginner's Gui
Video

Beginner's Guides are available on the following subjects:

Audio
Building Construction
Cameras
Central Heating
Colour Television
Computers
Digital Electronics
Domestic Plumbing
Electric Wiring
Electronics
Gemmology
Home Energy Saving
Integrated Circuits
Photography
Processing and Printing
Radio
Super 8 Film Making
Tape Recording
Television
Transistors
Woodturning
Woodworking

Beginner's Guide to
Video

David K. Matthewson

B.Sc., Ph.D., M.R.T.S.

Newnes Technical Books

Newnes Technical Books
is an imprint of the Butterworth Group
which has principal offices in
London, Boston, Durban, Singapore, Sydney, Toronto, Wellington

First published 1982
  Reprinted 1982

British Library Cataloguing in Publication Data

Matthewson, David K.
  Beginner's guide to video
  1. Video tape recorders and recording
  I. Title
  778.59'9   TK6655.V5

  ISBN 0-408-00577-7

Photoset by Butterworths Litho Preparation Department
Printed in England by Mansell Bookbinders Ltd, Witham, Essex

Preface

By the end of 1981 over 1 000 000 domestic type videotape recorders had been sold to the public in the United Kingdom, and yet it is only recently that the video recorder has become a mass marketed consumer electronic product.

Because of this, there is little serious information available to the intelligent 'man in the street' who wishes not only to understand how a video camera or recorder functions, but also how to get the best out of various items of video equipment.

This book is an attempt to rectify this deficiency and to remove some of the confusion surrounding the whole field of domestic video. Hopefully, those readers who do not yet own or rent any video equipment will find this book helpful in deciding what to buy, whilst those who possess equipment will gain a fuller understanding of its potential and thus increase their enjoyment of what is rapidly becoming a major recreational and communicational tool.

A large number of firms and individuals have co-operated in providing information, photographs and assistance without this book would not have been possible. Amongst others, these have included:

3M UK Ltd., 500 Video, Atari Ltd., BBC, BASF (UK) Ltd., British Telecom, CEL Electronics Ltd., Centronics Ltd., General Instrument Microelectronics Ltd., Ian Hirstle, Hitachi (UK) Ltd., IBA, ISE Ltd., ITT Consumer Products (UK) Ltd., JVC (UK) Ltd., Majorie Matthewson, Mitsubishi Electric (UK) Ltd., Mullard Ltd., National Panasonic Ltd., Philips Electrical Ltd., RCA Ltd., Sanyo Marubeni (UK) Ltd., Sharp Electronics (UK) Ltd., Sony (UK) Ltd., STC Ltd., Thorn Consumer Electronics Ltd., TMC Ltd., Toshiba (UK) Ltd., Videomaster Ltd., Kate Wall, CH Wood (Bradford) Ltd.

Any omissions and/or errors in the text are, of course, attributable to myself.

D.K.M.

Dedication

To my very own **Sus scrofa**

Contents

1 Television basics

Although this book is about video systems, it is useful to consider briefly the operating principles of conventional TV systems, and then to look at how these are applied to various items of TV equipment.

Fundamentals

Although we perceive a TV picture on our living room screens as a complete image it is in fact an illusion, built up by a very bright, rapidly moving pin-point of light. This dot of light is moving so rapidly that the persistence of vision of the human eye and brain combine the separate points of light into a complete picture. A TV cathode ray tube (CRT, also known as the picture tube) consists of an evacuated glass envelope, the inside face of which has been coated with a phosphor which glows when bombarded with electrons emitted by an electron gun situated at the far end of the tube. In a black and white TV tube a monochromatic phosphor is used, which gives off white light and in a colour tube separate red, green and blue phosphors are used. (In the correct combinations light from these can be of almost any desired colour.)

The electron beam which illuminates the tube is produced by an electron gun in a manner very similar to that used in any thermionic valve (see *Figure 1.1*).

If that were all there was to a CRT then the result would be a single spot of light at the centre of the screen, rather than the familiar image. Some means of moving the spot about the tube in a controlled manner is required and this is normally achieved by

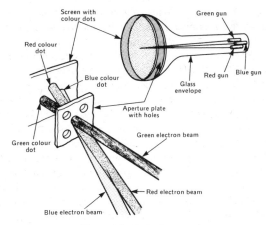

Figure 1.1. Cathode ray tube

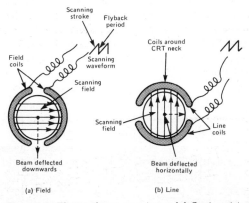

Figure 1.2. Electron beam scanning and deflection. (a) Showing vertical deflection. (b) Showing horizontal deflection

applying external magnetic fields through scanning coils. In practice two sets of coils are employed, one for line scanning (making the spot move from left to right and back again) and another for field scanning (moving the spot from the top to the bottom of the screen). When these two coils are used in conjunction the scanning spot may be moved in a precisely controlled manner (see *Figure 1.2*).

Mainly for historical reasons the line scanning rate on UK 625 line (colour) TV is 15.625 kHz and the field scanning rate 50 Hz. In other words, as the vertical repetition rate is 50 Hz, a complete set of lines forming the raster must appear every 1/50 second (20 ms). As the line frequency is 15.625 kHz, there must be 15 625/50 = 312.5 lines per vertical scan. This seems odd, as it is well known that colour TV in the UK is transmitted on 625 lines. The answer is that each TV picture is composed of two vertical scans, each having half the number of lines of the complete picture. So a complete TV picture is produced every 1/25 second (40 ms) and is said to consist of two fields, providing one frame of interlaced picture. *(Figure 1.3)*. Interlacing is a way of fitting the two fields together to form a picture and is done to increase the horizontal definition without increasing the band-width of the signal. (This means that the amount of frequency spectrum occupied by the transmitted signal is not too large.)

Having looked at the basics of the way in which the TV picture is built up, let us now look at some of the other parts of a domestic TV set.

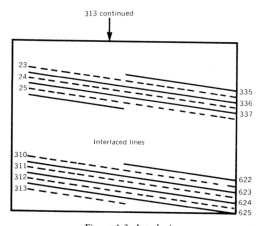

Figure 1.3. Interlacing

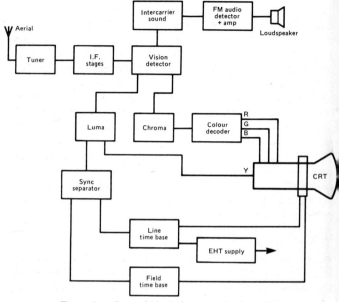

Figure 1.4. General block diagram of colour TV

Most of the parts shown in *Figure 1.4* are self-explanatory, but here and there a few words of explanation are in order.

The TV tuner and IF stages have the task of receiving the broadcast signals and, regardless of the exact transmission frequency, turning them into two common frequencies. In the UK these are 39.5 MHz for the vision and 33.5 MHz for the sound signal. The sound and vision signals can be separated from each other as they are transmitted on different frequencies. For example, my local transmitter at Emley Moor has the following frequencies:

	Sound MHz	Vision MHz	Channel
BBC 1	661.25	655.25	44
BBC 2	717.25	711.25	51
ITV 1	685.25	679.25	47
ITV 2	637.25	631.25	41

You will note that the sound and vision carriers are always in the UK separated by 6 MHz. This is one standard of the international convention CCIR (Comité Consultatif International des Radiocommunications). This technique is called the intercarrier sound system. The separated sound signal can then be passed to a FM detector and on to an amplifier and loudspeaker. The vision signal is also fed from the IFs to a vision detector, where chroma (colour) and luma (luminance) information are detected and filtered out. The luma signal has little further processing to undergo before it is fed to the TV tube, although it must be used to provide information for the timebase (scanning) circuits which move the electron beam. This is achieved by separating the line and field synchronising pulses from the rest of the video signal, and at this point it seems opportune to examine the video waveform in more detail.

Video waveform

If you hooked an oscilloscope to the output of the vision detector in a TV set displaying colour bars, a waveform something like the one shown in *Figure 1.5* would be observed. If only a grey

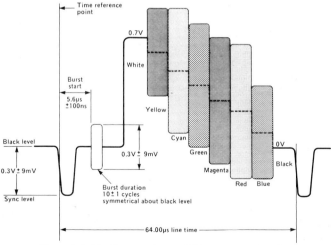

Figure 1.5. The line waveform of 100 per cent colour bars

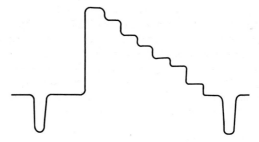

Figure 1.6. Black and white waveform

scale (no colour) was being transmitted then the waveform
would look like *Figure 1.6.* Both these waveforms represent one
TV line, that is, the information required to move the electron
beam across the screen and to modulate it to produce light and
dark areas. The amplitude (height) of the signal increases as the
whiteness of the scene increases. In other words, a totally white
object filling the screen would look like *Figure 1.7 (a)* and a
totally black one like *Figure 1.7 (b).*

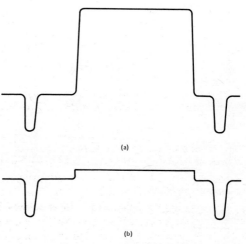

(a)

(b)

Figure 1.7. Waveforms. (a) Peak white. (b) Black level

The pulses descending below true black level are the line synchronising pulses which instruct the CRT scanning coils that a complete line has been scanned and that the spot should return to the lefthand side to start a new line. This sequence will be repeated for 312½ lines, when it will be necessary to send the spot from the bottom right of the screen to the top left. This occurs during the field synchronising period and is initiated by the field pulses (see *Figure 1.8*).

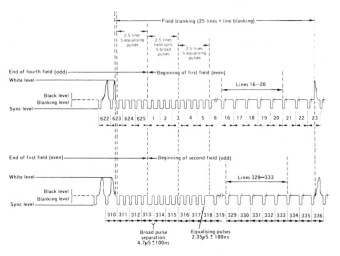

Figure 1.8. Odd and even fields. Vertical synchronising and blanking waveforms for a typical signal. Lines 7–14 and 320–327 have been omitted

In the receiver these two sets of pulses, line and field, are extracted from the video signal and used to drive the line and field scanning circuits. This separation is achieved by a sync separator circuit, which differentiates out the line pulses and integrates and separates the field pulses. This is possible because (a) the pulse lengths are very different and (b) there is a *series* of field pulses. These pulses are then shaped and used to drive the line and field output stages, which control the scanning beam.

Luminance and chrominance

It is in this area that the main differences between colour and black and white television occur.

The luminance (black and white) information is carried as changes in amplitude of the video waveform, but the chrominance (colour) information is carried on top of the luminance signal in the form of a modulated high frequency (4.43 MHz) signal. This will be seen in more detail in the section on television standards.

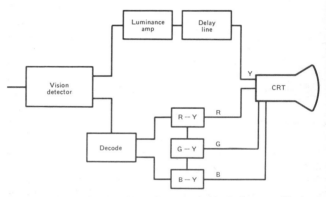

Figure 1.9. Typical colour TV colour circuit block diagram. The luma delay is to ensure that the luma and chroma signals arrive at the tube simultaneously, as the chroma processing delays the signal more than the luma

This chroma information is easily separated from the luminance by means of high pass filters which let it through but not the luminance. Having extracted the chrominance it is now necessary to decode it into red, green and blue signals, which are applied to the red, green and blue electron guns of the colour tube (*Figure 1.9*).

Television standards

One of the continuing problems in television is that brought about by the different, incompatible, TV standards which have been adopted throughout the world. Although originally only a problem to the broadcasters, this lack of standardisation is now affecting owners of domestic video tape recorders (VTRs). For example, tapes produced in the USA cannot be replayed on UK VTRs and vice versa. Let us look at the background to the problem and see how it can be overcome. It must be stressed that in this and in the following section we are only looking at *video* signal standards, as opposed to the RF systems used in the various countries to transmit signals to viewer's TV screens.

In fact there are two problems involved: the line standard (number of scanning lines needed to form a complete picture) and the colour standards used (how the colour information is transmitted). As the line standard difference is the older one, that will be examined first.

Line standards

We have already seen that in the UK 625 horizontal lines are employed to produce a complete TV picture, these being transmitted as two fields, each of 312½ lines. The two fields form a frame, and the frame repitition rate is 25 Hz; in other words 25 frames, or complete pictures, are transmitted every second. It can be seen that the field frequency must therefore be 50 Hz and the line frequency 15.625 kHz. The choice of 50 Hz stems from early television experiments when the 50 Hz mains were used to lock the field oscillator. Today this is no longer the case, and the picture transmissions are said to be asynchronous with the mains frequency.

In the USA, again for historical reasons, the mains frequency of 60 Hz was initially used to lock the field oscillator and 525, rather than 625 lines were used to form a complete picture. These figures give rise to a line frequency of 15.75 kHz, with a normal 2:1 interlaced picture and a frame frequency of 30 Hz, giving 30 pictures per second. It can be seen that even in black and white it will not be possible to display correctly 525 lines/60 Hz pictures on a UK 625 lines/50 Hz television without some considerable modifications being undertaken. The situation in

Europe is slightly simpler if one forgets the now obsolete UK 405 lines and French 819 lines systems, and looks at black and white pictures only. In this case the video standards employed are compatible and a black and white video tape recorded in the UK will play back satisfactorily in France or Germany.

Colour standards

There are three incompatible colour standards. The oldest is the American NTSC system, so-called because it was devised by the National Television Standards Committee, set up originally to determine the monochrome system to be adopted, and re-formed in 1950 to deliberate on the colour system the USA should use.

By the end of 1953 a system had been adopted and put into use. As with all colour TV systems to date it had to be compatible with black and white transmissions and receivers, so that existing black and white sets could still receive a colour signal although displaying it in black and white only. For technical reasons this could only be achieved by slightly altering the line frequency to 15.73426 kHz and the field frequency to 58.94 Hz. These values were so close to those originally employed that existing black and white sets continued to function adequately.

NTSC   This colour system is of the simultaneous type; that is, information concerning all three primary colours (red, green and blue) is transmitted together. The use of red, green and blue components allows any possible colour to be formed by the mixing of the primaries in the correct proportions. A three-tube television camera, one tube looking through a coloured filter for each primary colour, will produce a suitable signal which will then need to be encoded for transmission. In theory it is possible to transmit just the red, just the green and just the blue information and combine them in the receiver, but this would not be compatible with black and white receivers and would occupy too much signal bandwidth. Broadly speaking, in the NTSC system the colour information is transmitted as two colour difference signals, which are used to modulate a high frequency colour subcarrier which 'sits' on top of the luminance (black and white) signal. In this system a subcarrier of 3.579545 MHz is employed.

The TV receiver has to decode the received subcarrier back into its component primary colours, which are used to drive the red, green and blue guns of a colour CRT. To do this it is essential that the receiver decoder can lock into phase with the transmitter encoder. If this were not to occur, more or less random colour would be produced. This synchronisation is achieved by transmitting a small burst of subcarrier at the beginning of each line of video information. This allows the local oscillator in the receiver to be in synchronisation with that at the transmitter encoder and ensures that the colours are correctly displayed (see *Figure 1.10*).

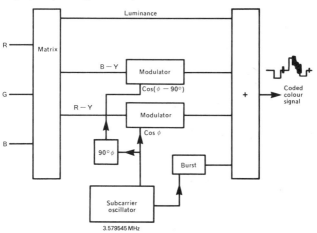

Figure 1.10. NTSC coder block diagram

That really sums up the basics of the NTSC colour system and if it seems familiar to those acquainted with the British PAL system this is because PAL is a derivation of NTSC.

Pal colour   The PAL (Phase Alternate Line) colour system is essentially a superior version of the NTSC system. As with NTSC the colour information is carried in the form of a high frequency (4.43 MHz) signal superimposed on the luminance signal.

The main differences between the two colour systems are:

(1) The subcarrier of the R-Y signal is phase reversed line by line. In NTSC systems this phase reversal does not occur.

(2) The phase of the colour burst is also switched line by line, so that the receiver local oscillator can be provided with the necessary information about the R-Y chroma signal.

(3) In the receiver a one-line delay line is employed to allow phase errors which occur in transmission to be considerably reduced. A form of PAL called PAL-S (Simple) does not use a delay line and relies on the viewers' eyes averaging errors between lines.

(4) A different subcarrier frequency is used.

It is generally agreed that the PAL system is superior to the NTSC one, because of its high immunity to phase-related line

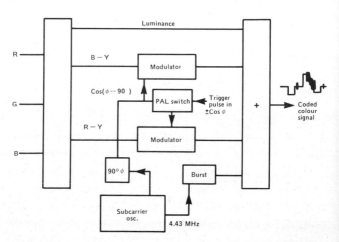

Figure 1.11. PAL coder. The PAL switch reverses phase at the start of each line

errors, which are often induced by multipath reception; that is, echoes from hills, buildings and other objects (see *Figure 1.11*). When the PAL signal is received by the TV it needs to be decoded back into luma and RGB signals to drive the CRT. This is achieved as shown in *Figure 1.12*. An NTSC decoder would appear almost identical, but with a 3.58 MHz oscillator and no PAL switch section or reference oscillator phase shift. The effect

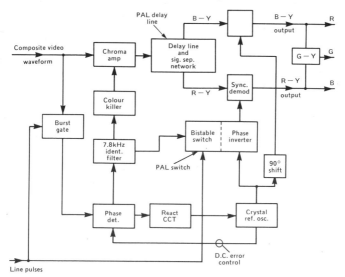

Figure 1.12. PAL decoder block diagram

of this phase shift is to cancel out phase errors which occur in adjacent lines, due to signal ghosting caused by multipath reception.

SECAM   The French system for colour television is quite different from both NTSC and PAL, and is of the sequential type; that is, not all the information concerning the red, green and blue colours is transmitted at one time. SECAM stands for Séquential Couleur à Mémoire, and has been adopted not only by France and its former colonies (Algeria and Tunisia) but also the USSR and its client states, amongst others.

To retain compatibility between black and white and colour transmissions, SECAM colour information is transmitted as a subcarrier which is frequency modulated by colour difference signals, R–Y and B–Y. These signals are transmitted sequentially. The phase of the chroma signal is irrelevant in SECAM, as the decoding relies on the sub-carrier frequency, rather than the phase. In the receiver an electronic delay line and switch are used to ensure that both R–Y and B–Y signals arrive at the CRT at the same time, to produce a normal colour picture.

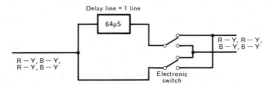

Figure 1.13. SECAM decoder block diagram

The advantages of SECAM are based around having a simpler receiver than PAL or NTSC and having an immunity to phase problems, which afflicts NTSC but not PAL. These advantages are outweighed by the disadvantage caused in studio work by having a sequential colour system. Vision mixing in SECAM is not possible without decoding the signal to RGB and then recoding it. See *Figure 1.13*. There are, in fact, two types of SECAM used, called horizontal and vertical. These differences apply only to the transmitted RF signal and not to the video level signal so they need not concern us here.

Television transmission

Having looked at the three colour systems, let us now see how these are transmitted in different countries and how this affects

VTR owners and users. As if two different line and field standards (USA and the rest) and three colour standards (NTSC, PAL and SECAM) were not enough, there are a large number of different, incompatible, ways of transmitting TV sound and vision. The CCIR controls which system is used in which country.

Television transmission is very similar to radio transmission in that a high frequency carrier signal is modulated by changes in amplitude of a control signal. In a sound system this control system is the audio output from a studio, etc., whereas for TV it is the video signal. As it is necessary to pack as many TV channels into the available spectrum as possible, a system called vestigial sideband transmission is used. In this the lower sideband of the signal is considerably reduced by filters.

The TV sound signal is transmitted on a slightly different frequency from that of the vision, and it is here that one of the major incompatibilities occurs. The separation between sound and vision is very important, as in receivers it allows sound and vision to be processed separately. In the UK we have adopted what is called Comité Consultatif International des Radiocommunications (CCIR) standard I, which means that the bandwidth of a complete TV channel is 8 MHz, with the upper sideband of the vision signal occupying 5.5 MHz, the lower one 1.25 MHz,

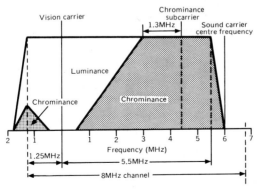

Figure 1.14. RF spectrum from a CCIR PAL I transmitter

and the sound signal 14 KHz. The sound carrier is located 6 MHz above the vision carrier. See *Figure 1.14*.

Other countries have adopted a range of transmission standards, so that even though they may be using the same line and colour standards, a TV receiver (or off-air domestic VTR) in one country will not necessarily receive programmes transmitted in another. The most common difference is that of the sound–to–vision spacing. In the UK it is 6 MHz, whereas in continental Europe a value of 5.5 MHz has been adopted (CCIR type B) and in the USA it is 4.5 MHz. This means that, for example, a German VTR when used off-air in the UK will record the vision signal but not the sound. There are over 14 different TV transmission standards in use around the world, and as a rule, a TV set or off-air VTR designed solely for one system will not work with any other. *Table 1.1* lists some of the characteristics of the principal systems. Generally speaking, PAL colour is used on systems B, D, G, I, SECAM on K and L and NTSC on M.

It must be re-emphasised that these differences are transmitter characteristics and do not affect the video signal parameters and consequently what is recorded on video tape. How all these various factors affect the international use of video tapes and equipment, and how some of the problems are circumvented, will now be examined.

Standards differences and video tape compatibility

Leaving aside the colour differences, let us suppose that a UK VTR owner wishes to purchase an American video cassette of, say, 'Star Wars'. If he owns a JVC HR 3336 video cassette recorder, he may well imagine that if he purchases an American VHS (Video Home System) pre-recorded tape then he will have the right tape. Unfortunately this is not so, for the American tape will have been recorded to the NTSC 525 lines/60 fields standard and will not even run at the correct speed in a UK VTR, let alone give a picture. The converse is also true of course.

Table 1.1. Characteristics of the principal TV systems

Country	Colour	CCIR system	Number of lines	Vision mod	Field frequency Hz	Sound mod	Sound/vision separation MHz	Total channel width MHz	Vision channel width MHz
UK	PAL	I	625	–	50	FM	+6.0	8	5.5
USA & Japan	NTSC	M	525	–	60	FM	+4.5	6	4.2
		B	625	–	50	FM	+5.5	7	3
W. Germany	PAL	G	625	–	50	FM	+5.5	8	5
France	SECAM	L	625	+	50	AM	+6.5	8	6
		D	625	–	50	FM	+6.5	8	6
USSR	SECAM	K	625	–	50	FM	+6.5	8	6
Brazil	PAL	M	525	–	60	FM	+4.5	6	4.2

With SECAM the problem is slightly easier, for if a SECAM tape is played on a UK VTR, a black and white only picture will be produced. The converse also applies. This is because the line standards are the same for PAL and SECAM. It is unfortunate that the VHS specification for SECAM standard recorders differs between those intended for France and the Middle East SECAM areas. As a result a further incompatibility has been introduced. Of course, a SECAM tape cannot be played on an NTSC machine and vice versa. These apparently insoluble problems affect not only domestic users, but also the broadcasters.

It is this market which has brought about one of the two means of overcoming the standard problem, namely the standards conversion machine. These are really two main ways of turning NTSC 525 lines pictures into PAL 625 lines and vice versa. The first is to use optical methods; that is, basically playing the tape on an NTSC outfit, and shooting the monitor with a PAL camera. The results from broadcast standard installations of this type can be very good, but there are considerable problems to overcome. A better way of conversion is to employ a digital standards convertor, which breaks down the picture into a digital form, stores it in a memory and reads it out at a different line standard. Extra lines (for 525 to 625) can be generated by repeating existing ones or omitted (for 625 to 525) as required. The results from these machines are excellent, but their purchase price is very high, making even hiring time on them very expensive. For the non-broadcast market, a cheaper way of allowing tape interchange is required and it is here that the multi-standard VTR has found a niche.

Basically these machines allow tapes produced to several line and colour standards to be replayed on modified television sets. The first of this type to appear in the UK was the SONY VO-181OP, a ¾ inch U-matic format machine designed to record and play back UK PAL tapes and replay only NTSC tapes. This was achieved by the use of additional circuitry, which altered the tape speed as well as the colour signal processing. To make this an economic proposition, the resultant 525 lines 60 Hz NTSC signal in fact had a colour subcarrier of 4.43 MHz, instead of the NTSC standard of 3.53 MHz. Not only did this reduce the additional circuitry in the VTR, and hence the cost, but it also meant that a reasonably conventional UK PAL TV set could be used to display the picture. Sony produced a range of TV monitor/receivers which automatically altered the frame scanning rate from PAL to NTSC standards and disabled the PAL delay line circuitry to enable NTSC colour to be displayed. Various other manufacturers, notably BARCO, and JVC, also produced similar dual-standard TV receivers. VTRs which could replay SECAM tapes as well as PAL and NTSC followed, with Sony's U-matic 2060 which records both PAL and SECAM signals and plays them back, as well as NTSC 4.43 signals. Suitable triple-standard monitors are also available.

However, the U-matic range of recorders is not really suitable for domestic use and first purpose-built multi-standard domestic VTR is also from Sony, the SLT-7ME. This Beta format VTR will record SECAM and PAL signals and replay them, as well as replaying NTSC ones. A VHS multi-standard VTR is available in a version of the Sharp VC 6300, but again this will not record NTSC. Interestingly, several small specialist firms such as Teletape, REW and Portatel will modify both VHS and Beta VTRs to record and replay every standard of tape, so if a true triple-standard VTR is a must for you, then around £1200 (at 1981 prices) will buy a suitable machine and receiver/monitor. Sony market relatively low-cost (less than £1000) devices for PAL to SECAM, and vice versa, transcoding and NTSC 4.43 to NTSC 3.56, and vice versa, transcoding.

Receiver/monitors

In this chapter receiver/monitors have been mentioned several times, and the term will recur at frequent intervals throughout the book, so let us see how these differ from normal TV sets.

A conventional TV set is designed to receive a signal from an aerial and translate it into sound and vision display. A receiver/monitor will also do this, but will also make the sound and vision signals available at a socket on the set body at a suitable level and impedance for recording on a VTR. Similarly the receiver/

monitor will also accept sound and vision signals from a VTR and display them. In this way a higher quality display is achieved as the VTR modulator and TV tuner are bypassed. Generally speaking, a receiver/monitor will be a normal TV set with the addition of some buffer amplifiers and a mains isolating transformer. The latter is essential as most domestic TVs have a 'live chassis' with one side of the 240 V AC supply connected to the chassis. Without an isolation transformer anyone touching the metal chassis could receive a fatal shock. A receiver/monitor will cost upwards of around £100 (UK 1980 prices) on top of the price for the basic TV (see *Figure 1.15*).

There also exists what are called monitors, which as the name implies, are capable of displaying only the vision (and sometimes sound) signal which is fed into them from a camera or VTR. Although common in professional broadcasting facilities they are unlikely to occur in the domestic environment.

Contemporary TV sets have a wide range of features which would have been unthinkable only 10 years ago. Almost all sets

Figure 1.15. JVC CX 610GB portable colour TV, capable of displaying PAL and SECAM pictures. It can also be used as a video monitor (JVC)

now have a pre-selector channel marked either 'AV' or 'VTR/ VCR', which is the preferred channel when using them with a VTR. This is because the synchronising signal from a domestic VTR is often not up to the standard of the broadcasting equipment for which the set is primarily designed and will result in picture roll or 'hooking' at the top of the screen. The AV channel selector alters the timebase constant in the TV set to overcome this. Other interesting developments have included full remote control, initially with ultrasonic–based systems, but more recently using infra-red controllers. These do not drive the dog up the wall!

Sets capable of receiving various videotext services are becoming fairly common, with prices falling quite rapidly. Some sets are now equipped with built-in TV game units, radio, and cassette recorders. A recent model from Pye also incorporated a digital clock.

On the technical side, an interesting development by various European and Japanese manufacturers has been to incorporate a

Figure 1.16. An experimental voice-activated, voice-response TV from Toshiba (Toshiba)

small (say 6 inch) black and white picture of another TV channel
in the top corner of the main 26 inch colour screen. This allows a
viewer to monitor one channel whilst watching another. This
type of display relies on computer memory technology and is
expensive to produce. Its entertainment value is felt to be
limited. A very recent development has been to have the
inserted picture in colour.

Another technical advance has been the demonstration of
various sets which are controlled by voice command and even
reply, verbally, to a command. A model from Toshiba will
accept 'On', 'Off' and 'Change channel' and replies 'OK' or

*Figure 1.17. Sony KV 2704UB, the largest screen domestic TV set on sale
in Europe, which can also be used as a video monitor (Sony)*

'Repeat, please'. Again, although technically impressive, the value of this development is rather obscure.

TV sound has, in the past, been considered as the poor relation to the picture, but recent developments have changed this, with some Philips and Bang and Olufsen sets being capable of giving true hi-fi sound. In Europe and Japan true TV stereo sound is being transmitted and we can hope for a similar development in the UK.

When you consider that in 1953 a 9 inch black and white TV set cost around 50 guineas (£52.50) and that a modern black and white portable today also costs around £50–£60, the world of video can only be seen as becoming more affordable!

2 Large-screen, projection and flat-screen television

The largest common size of televisions available are those with 26 inch diagonal screens – 32 inch ones are being manufactured, but they are very expensive and not likely to become common in domestic use for a while yet. To obtain larger-sized pictures some form of either projection or flat-screen television is needed. Projection is not, in fact, a new idea, as it was seen as a way of producing television pictures watchable by a complete family when television sets were first produced in the 1950s. In those early days the largest cathode ray tubes were either five or nine inches across and several manufacturers built them into projection units. The Philips 6028 of 1952 was reasonably typical, looking like a radiogram, with a separate screen complete with built-in loud speaker. A single five inch tube projected the image on to the set lid where a mirror reflected it on to the three foot diagonal screen which was placed about five feet away. The whole, rather bulky, affair needed almost total darkness to work in and even then the black and white picture was rather vague and dim.

Once larger cathode ray tubes began to become available these early projection televisions died out and it is only in recent years that interest in domestic projection television has been rekindled. However, there is another market for projection television outside the home and that is for cinema-like purposes. For this large, 30-foot, screens with a bright image are required. Just before the last war a research team in Switzerland started to develop the Eidophor projector which has been used for many years in all those applications where very large pictures are required. This machine is now available in both black and white and colour forms but the latter costing around £250,000: not exactly domestic equipment. These projectors have found use in NASA's mission control and also for showing Muhammed Ali's prize-fights and similar high value sporting events, as well as at rock concerts, television studios, etc. Something much cheaper is needed for use in the home, and there are two current lines of research in this field. As well as various small projection units, some of which have reached the market, there are also some genuine flat-screen television units which are very thin complete television sets. The development of these latter units is quite exciting as a true flat-screen television would be used not only for a wall-mounted set but also for portable pocket sets.

Technical principles

The simplest way of projecting a black and white image is that employed in the 1950s sets; the CRT is used along with a mirror to throw an image on to a screen. The problem with this approach is that the resulting picture is very dull; it cannot be any brighter on the screen than it is on the front of the CRT. Often the cathode ray tube EHT is over-run to produce a brighter-than-average picture but as this shortens the tube life it is not a very satisfactory solution. One of the earliest domestic colour video projectors which used this system was the Sony VPP-200, employing a modified 13-inch Trinitron tube and a 4-foot screen. Again it suffered from the same problems, although it used a metallised reflector screen to try and improve the dim picture. These screens are very common and are used in all current projectors. They consist of an aluminised metal screen attached to a glass fibre backing. The whole screen is slightly curved, and although they do reflect more light and thus give a brighter picture than plain screens, they have a narrow viewing angle so that you have to sit almost in line with the

projector. In an attempt to improve the light output other types
of optical system have been designed.

Figure 2.1 shows the four systems which have been proposed
for domestic large-screen television – the Eidophor system is not
a domestic one. Historically, the external Schmidt optical system
was the first to be developed, originally for black and white
work. In this system a high-intensity CRT 3 to 5 inch diameter
throws an image at a spherical mirror which reflects it back past
the cathode ray tube through a corrective lens and onto the
screen. The larger the mirror, the brighter the image on the
screen. For colour work three CRTs are used, red, green and
blue, each with its own mirror. The whole assembly is arranged
so that a converged, focused image is projected onto a screen at
a fixed distance from the projection unit. As can be readily
appreciated the mechanical aspects of this system tend to make it
rather expensive and difficult to align and maintain.

The next development was the internal Schmidt tube, initially
deployed in the Advent Corporation Video Beam 1000 A. Here
a mirror and lens are incorporated into the CRT envelope thus
much simplifying the alignment problem. A small hole in the
spherical mirror through which the electron beam enters does
not detract noticeably from the image because of its small size in
relation to the image distance. The Video Beam 1000 A employed three internal Schmidt tubes, (one for each of the
primary colours) and threw the colour image onto a 7-foot
diagonal screen. The focusing was very restricted and the screen
had to be exactly 10 feet from the projector.

We have already briefly mentioned the Trinitron reflective
system which is still produced by various manufacturers, now
employing other in-line tubes as well as the Trinitron. These
systems allow a more or less unmodified TV to be equipped with
an add-on lens and turned into a low-cost projection television.
All that needs to be done is to reverse the scan coils so that the
image on the screen is seen the right way round. The problem is
that, besides not looking very elegant, the resulting picture is
very dim. Again the projected image cannot be any brighter than
that on the cathode ray screen – which might be acceptable at 13
inches across but is less so at 60 inches. The highly reflective

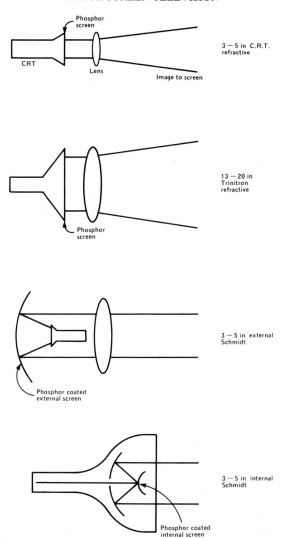

Figure 2.1. Domestic large-screen projection systems

metallised screens mentioned above are an absolute necessity with these systems. As only a single CRT is employed there are no problems of convergence – aligning the three separate colour images – which can occur with separate tube units.

Moving away from this very simple approach, some manufacturers have used three separate CRTs in a refractive, as opposed to a reflective, that is, Schmidt unit. The cost of manufacturing conventional CRTs is a lot less than that of Schmidt tubes, so the whole price tends to be cheaper. The Video Beam 750 uses this system, with three 5-inch diameter CRTs, again one for each colour. Lenses focus the images to converge onto a screen at a fixed distance from the projector. However, you never get something for nothing so the lower cost of the refractive system is reflected in the low light output and consequently a dimmer picture.

An attempt to overcome this problem is shown by the Aquabeam about which there has been much talk but little action, at least in the UK. This system employs three CRTs bonded on to a transparent box containing two dichroic mirrors (reflecting specified wave lengths – colours – of light only) and highly refractive liquid. This liquid is also used to cool the cathode ray tubes and thus allows them to be run at higher outputs than normal. The system has considerable theoretical potential and it will be interesting to see if it can be marketed successfully.

The professional Eidophor system *(Figure 2.2)* manages to project such a bright image (3600 lux) either in black and white or colour, because it does not rely on a cathode ray tube as the illuminating force. Instead a xenon arc lamp, similar to that used in many cinema projectors is used. This light is transmitted through a device known as a 'light valve'. This is essentially a very thin layer of oil over a mirrored surface. The oil is bombarded by an electron beam from a CRT which deforms it, allowing the light from the arch lamp to pass through and be projected onto the screen. For a black and white system a single xenon lamp and light valve is used but for colour systems three are needed, filtered to give red, green and blue images. Of course in practice a lot more electronics and optics are involved

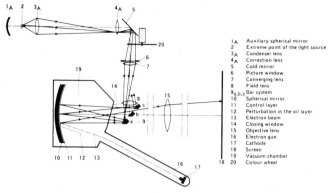

1A	Auxiliary spherical mirror
2	Extreme point of the light source
3A	Condenser lens
4A	Correction lens
5	Cold mirror
6	Picture window
7	Converging lens
8	Field lens
9a,b,c	Bar system
10	Spherical mirror
11	Control layer
12	Perturbation in the oil layer
13	Electron beam
14	Closing window
15	Objective lens
16	Electron gun
17	Cathode
18	Screen
19	Vacuum chamber
20	Colour wheel

Figure 2.2. Basic operating principle of the Eidophor large-screen projector. A colour version consists of three separate projection tubes, one for each primary colour

but the general principle is still true. The very high light output allows back projection techniques in quite well-lit rooms to be employed.

The final system proposed for large-screen television is not based on projection at all but on a conventional CRT bent in an unusual way and known as the Gabor tube. Developed initially in the 1950s and then abandoned, the Gabor tube was a UK invention designed to try and get round the problems of the early small-diameter cathode ray tubes. Once larger CRTs could be made the Gabor was dropped. Sinclair Electronics picked up the idea again in the 1970s and developed it to use in their TV 2 portable, pocket-sized radio/television set *(Figure 2.3)*. As can be seen from the accompanying diagrams the device is basically a conventional cathode ray tube but bent in such a way as to make it very thin. Although initially used in pocket sets, this tube has considerable attractions for use as a wall-hanging, large-screen television unit as it is only about two inches thick. Again it is available in black and white only so far but presents no insuperable problems for colour use. Image brightness is not a problem in this system as the image is seen from the same side of the phosphor screen as that which the electron beam scans and

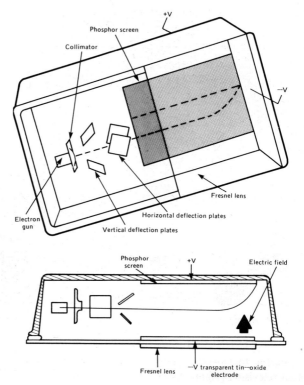

Figure 2.3. Gabor type tube as used by Sinclair

strikes. In fact, an image about three times brighter can be obtained for about one-eighth of the power requirements of a conventional CRT.

Flat-screen television

Liquid crystal, light-emitting diode and plasma technologies are of interest for small flat-screen black and white portable units,

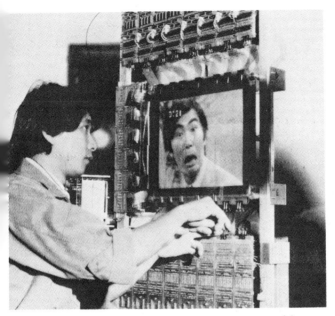

Figure 2.4. An experimental flat-screen TV from a Japanese laboratory (Matsushita)

but appear to have insuperable problems when it comes to colour television *(Figure 2.4)*.

Uses of large-screen television

Before some of the currently-available projection television units are discussed it will be helpful to look at some of the uses to which large-screen television can be put and also to mention some of the advantages – and associated problems.

Starting at the cheapest end of the market, domestic users are slowly beginning to purchase the more basic units for genuine use in the home, although this is seen as a very limited market as the price of around £1500 (in 1980) is still rather expensive. A problem briefly mentioned earlier is that none of the projection units, whether the earlier separate screen and projector models or the later combined units, is particularly elegant and thus will not fit comfortably into many modern flats and homes.

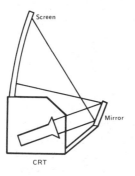

Figure 2.5. Schematic arrangement of a self-contained projection unit, using internal Schmidt optics

The educational/training sector is moving more rapidly into projection television for use mainly in showing video-taped programmes to large audiences. It is here that some of the £2000/£4000 units such as those from National, Sony and Advent are being used. Unfortunately, the curved, highly reflective, metallised screens these sets employ limit the viewing area quite considerably. Whilst this is not a problem for up to six people only, around a 45° arc of acceptable picture viewing. This cannot, unfortunately, be overcome without increasing the light output of the projector and using a conventional film projection screen. This of course increases the cost. It is instructive to realise that an average 16 millimetre film projector produces around 500 to 700 lux of illumination, whereas the simple Trinitron projectors produce around 15 to 20 lux. Three-tube refractive units give around 50 to 80 lux with external Schmidt systems giving around 90 to 120 lux.

Moving into true commercial markets, television projection units have found favour in some cinemas, with special interest films. The EMI ABC 4 in Norwich was one of the first cinemas in the UK to adopt television projection. The reason for this is one of cost-saving, both in terms of the equipment involved and the costs of a film print as compared with the video cassette copy. The production costs in 1980 of a 35 millimetre commercial print are around £600 as compared to £100 for video cassette copy. About 80 to 100 people is the maximum audience.

In-flight television

Recently some of the international airlines have replaced their in-flight film projection equipment with video cassette players linked to projection television units. This is mainly due to the increased reliability of projection television units with no moving parts, compared with the 16 millimetre film projectors. All-Nippon Airways, of Japan, have recently installed special solid state television cameras made by Sony in the cockpits of some of their own airliners linked to projection TV facilities in the cabin. This allows passengers to watch the take-offs and landings of the aircraft. TV stations have, and will continue to use, large-screen television units; here though we are talking about the professional Eidophor system.

Typical models

Having looked at the background to large-screen television systems and some of the history involved let us now look at some of the examples currently available.

The Dynavision Projection TV unit available for around £400 is reasonably typical of the Trinitron or similar projectors. This device is essentially an add-on lens attached to the front of an existing 12 to 20 inch television set. The set needs modifying to reverse the image on the tube – an easy modification which can be controlled by a single switch. The lens is held on to the television set by strips of Velcro-like material that allows it to be removed for ordinary TV watching. The whole assembly, television and lens, sits on a low, tilted table and is pointed at a four foot diagonal screen situated about eight feet away. Focusing is achieved by altering the set-to-screen distance, the fine focus being obtained on the adjustable two-part fresnel lens system. The screen is a highly reflective one with a gain of about three times and has approximately a 60° arc of view. Even so, almost total darkness is needed to provide an acceptable picture. Also a separate screen and projector do not make for very easy focusing. However, at around £400 plus the cost of a television set, it must be the cheapest projection television unit on the market.

Complete units

Next up the scale of costs are the combined units made by Sony, Mitsubishi and National as well as some other makers. These are complete units incorporating a projector and screen in a single housing as well as a television tuner unit. All you need is a television aerial and a mains plug. The National Panasonic Cinema Vision at around £2500 is reasonably typical, with a 60 inch diagonal screen. A maximum brightness of around 50 lux is possible so it is feasible to watch it in subdued lighting rather than no light at all. Three internal Schmidt tubes are employed which, along with a built-in convergence test circuit (a cross of red, green and blue lines projected onto the screen; if the convergence is correct a white image will appear, if not coloured fringes), ensure that high standards of focus and reliability are maintained. Built-in loudspeakers ensure excellent sound and the built-in television tuner has all the latest features including infra-red remote control, television station memory, on-screen channel number display, etc. A direct video input makes this projector ideal for use with a video cassette recorder. The use of a reflective screen again limits the horizontal viewing angle to about 60° with the vertical one being much smaller – about 10°. All in all, this is a well-designed and constructed unit which fills a gap in the luxury home and semi-professional market.

Figure 2.6. A back-projection large-screen TV unit for domestic use (Sanyo)

Predicting the future is always a risky business, but it is likely that the immediate future of large-screen television in the home will be based around a unit like the National, with a reduction in true cost. Indeed, since introducing it National have already

Figure 2.7. A front-projection large-screen TV incorporating a tuner and remote control (National)

Figure 2.8. National back-projection TV unit (National)

reduced the price by about £1000. In the longer term, true large flat-screen television will probably become a reality at reasonable cost. It will certainly be easier to install in many homes than projection TV.

The future

Finally, let us look at some of the experimental systems currently being developed for flat-screen television. Already mentioned has been the Sinclair TV 2, which, when marketed in 1981/2, will be the first true flat-screen television set, with a three-inch diagonal picture. In many ways it is similar in operation to a normal CRT. The tube is constructed from two sheets of glass, with a transparent front plate and a vacuum-moulded plastic back. The phosphor screen is deposited on the inside of the backing plate and the image is viewed through the transparent front screen. The electron gun assembly is mounted parallel to the phosphor and transparent front screens, but off-set to one side. Electrostatic deflection is used, there being in effect three sets of deflection electrodes. Two are conventional, giving vertical and horizontal deflection. The third set is of novel design and is used to deflect the beam onto the phosphor. Folding the electron beam in this way results in various types of picture distortion which are corrected by both electronic and optical means.

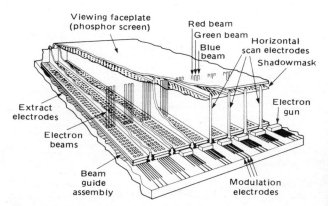

Figure 2.9. Proposed large-screen (50 inches) flat TV display from RCA. It is a variation on the Gabor type CRT, but with many separate electron guns

Though designed for black and white operation this principle can be applied to colour television as well. Sharp Electronics have recently demonstrated a flat-screen black and white set with a six inch diagonal screen, 2 inches thick. This uses an electroluminescent display and is not readily adaptable to colour signals. Other manufacturers have demonstrated prototypes using liquid crystal and light-emitting diode technologies but no one has announced sales dates for any flat-screen television set as yet. Future developments and research could result in a truly pocket-sized television set in the next five years or so.

3 Cameras

The price of both colour and black and white television cameras has fallen dramatically in the last few years, so much so that it is now, in 1980, possible to purchase a simple domestic colour camera for around £300. By domestic is meant a camera intended for taking 'home movies' and not really intended for proper television programme production. Generally these types of cameras are less sophisticated than their professional counterparts as well as being less robust. Just five years ago, the cheapest colour camera available would have cost ten times that amount and was aimed at the professional market. Along with this price reduction the design of both colour and black and white cameras has been simplified, a process which has been greatly aided by the use of integrated circuits.

In this chapter the basic component circuits of domestic cameras and how these have evolved from their professional studio counterparts will be discussed, and finally some of the more specialised cameras intended for security and scientific applications will be examined.

Basic building blocks

Any television camera whether professional or domestic, black and white or colour, has several features in common. Although we will be concentrating on domestic equipment it may be instructive to look at some professional equipment (See *Figure 3.1*) from which much domestic equipment has been developed. The heart of any camera is the tube which turns the incoming

Figure 3.1. A three-tube broadcast-type colour camera from Hitachi, type FPC 1000 (Ian Hirstle)

light into an electrical signal. Although many different types of camera tubes are available, all domestic types employ a tube called a vidicon.

The vidicon tube

The vidicon can be compared with a microphone, as they are both transducers which convert light and sound respectively into electrical voltages. It is the smallest of the various types of television tube, and is well suited to portable cameras. *Figure 3.2* shows a diagrammatic representation of a typical vidicon. Light from the image enters through the lens, and is focused on to the light-sensitive element of the tube. This is protected from the outside by a glass face plate. The light-sensitive part of the tube

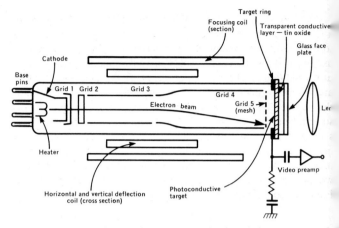

Figure 3.2. Sectional view of a conventional vidicon tube approximately 8 inches long by 1 inch diameter

or target disc, can be envisaged as an array of photo resistors one end of which is connected to the video preamplifier, and the electron beam thought of as the other contact of a complex switching system. The target disc is made from two electrically-separate parts; a conductive transparent film, usually tin oxide, on the inside of the glass face plate and a layer of photo-conductive material on the other, the scanning side. The resistance of the photo-conductive material, usually antimony trisulphide, decreases as light falls on it. This is a way of turning differences in light intensity into differences in resistance.

The problem now is to turn these difference in resistance into useful electrical signals. This is achieved by scanning the target with an electron beam, just as in a conventional CRT. The beam scans the target disc line by line, from top to bottom, and flies back to the top when the bottom is reached. When part of the target is brightly illuminated it has a comparatively low resistance, and thus a larger current flows than from a dark, high resistance area. Although this current is very small, about 1 to $4\mu A$, it is enough to be able to be amplified and processed into a video signal.

An interesting property of the vidicon tube is its ability to use a form of automatic sensitivity to enable its output to be altered to cope with the changes in lighting levels. This is particularly useful for domestic equipment which often has to give pictures under lighting conditions that are less then perfect. This is called auto target control, and is achieved by feeding a small sample of the output from the tube back to the target disc. The circuitry is so arranged that, as the tube output drops, the sampling circuits send an increasing signal to the target. As the target voltage is increased it becomes nore sensitive and thus the tube output increases. All we have looked at so far holds true for a vidicon whether it is used in a black and white or a colour camera. However some important differences now appear.

Tubes for colour cameras

A black and white camera merely has to detect changes in brightness, as does a black and white photographic film. Like a film, a camera tube ideally should respond in a similar manner to the human eye so they both 'see' the same thing. Although this is not strictly true, it is in most cases near enough. For use in a colour camera a tube, or tubes, has to achieve much more – just like its colour film counterpart. It not only has to reproduce the differences in brightness (luminance) but also the differences in colour (chroma) of the scene. There are several ways in which this can be achieved.

The simplest, historically the earliest but unfortunately the most expensive, is that adopted by some of the broadcast camera manufacturers. They built cameras using four vidicon-type tubes, one for the luminance, that is, the whole scene, and one for each of the primary colours. This can be achieved by the use

Y = yellow
M = magenta
C = cyan
W = white

Figure 3.3. Showing how the three primary colours, red, blue and green, can be added and subtracted to give magenta, cyan and white

of simple filters. *Figure 3.3* shows how red, green and blue can be added to produce a variety of colours. *Figure 3.4* shows a diagrammatic layout of a four-tube broadcast colour camera. A dichroic mirror is one which reflects light of a specified wavelength (colour) only. In practice dichroic prisms are used quite often in place of mirrors. Such a camera will give a very good colour rendering and sharp pictures, but will be very expensive and relatively bulky. The question is: how can it be reduced in size? It is possible to build a three-tube colour camera and also a two-tube one. A two-tube colour camera can be quite

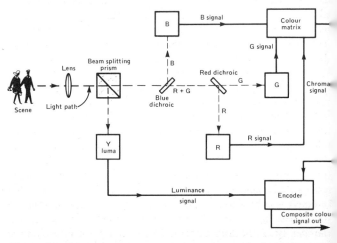

Figure 3.4. Diagrammatic representation of a professional four-tube colour camera, showing the three colour tubes (R, G and B) and the luminance (Y) tube. The dichroic filters pass certain specified colours only

portable and this approach has been adopted by a number of manufacturers including JVC and Philips. With modern two-thirds of an inch diameter vidicons, a hand-held portable colour camera is a practical proposition. However, two tubes can still lead to problems particularly in terms of registration. This is the phenomenon whereby the black and white image and the colour image do not quite coincide. As can be imagined, the problem can be much more tiresome with three- and four-tube cameras. Although registration adjustments are easy to make by means of altering the voltages on the tube scanning coils, they are time-consuming and best avoided on domestic equipment, where 'point and shoot' is a major criterion.

Single-tube colour cameras

For this reason the single-tube colour vidicom camera has proved very successful in the last few years. In these cameras a single vidicon is employed giving either separate or multiplexed red, green and blue outputs. ('Multiplexed' means one signal carrying several different 'chunks' of information; in this case colour information.) The luminance signal is obtained by combining a sample of each of these colour signals.

To get three separate colour outputs from a single tube is no mean feat and can be achieved by several means. One way is to use a rotary filter over the front of the tube. If the filter wheel has red, blue green segments then at any one moment the tube output would be all the reds, followed by all the blues, and then all the greens of the scene. Some sort of switching system would be needed along with a delay line to ensure that a proper red, green and blue signal is obtained. This could then be encoded into a PAL signal in the normal manner. If this seems a rather unlikely way of getting colour from a single vidicon, all that can be said is that a very similar system is used in the successful Ampex BC 210 colour camera. This employs two tubes, one of which looks at the luminance information and the other at the red and blue content of the picture. A rotary red and blue filter wheel is employed and a green signal is obtained by subtracting the red and blue signals from the luminance. However, such a system is not really suitable for portable domestic cameras, so two other approaches have been developed.

The first, developed by RCA and Sony amongst others, employs a single vidicon tube with a coloured filter face-plate bonded onto the front of the vidicon. This filter consists of yellow (that is white minus blue) and cyan (that is white minus

red) and clear stripes, arranged as shown in *Figure 3.5*. The tube
is otherwise a quite conventional vidicon; the electron beam
scans the target at the usual scanning speeds and the target
produes an output signal, the amplitude of which alters according to the rate at which the beam scans from the clear to the
coloured stripes. Thus the multiplexed colour signal, will be at a
relatively high frequency due to the large number of stripes. It
can thus easily be filtered from the lower frequency luminance
information. The high frequency signal is modulated by a colour
signal which is the difference between the luminance and either
the red or the blue parts of the scene. If the cyan and yellow

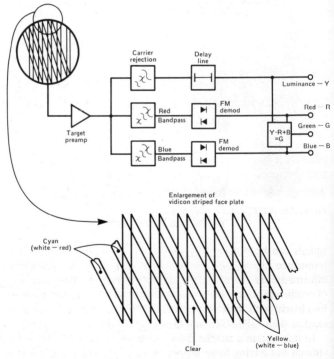

Figure 3.5. RCA spectraplex single-tube vidicon for colour cameras

stripes were arranged vertically then they would both produce carrier signals of the same frequency thus making it impossible to distinguish them. However, if one colour stripe is arranged vertically and the other diagonally at a different pitch, then two distinct frequencies result, one carrying red and the other blue information. These can be filtered and separated by band-pass filters and demodulated to produce red and blue signals. Green

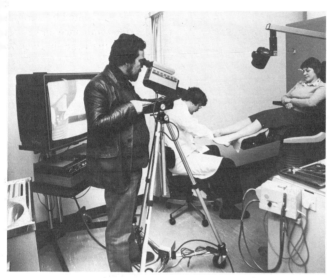

Figure 3.6. A GP5 colour camera in use in a chiropody clinic to produce a training tape (Ian Hirstle)

signals can be obtained by subtracting red and blue from the luminance signal, and the three colours and the luminance information are then processed in the usual way. The third way of producing acceptable colour from a single tube is that adopted by Hitachi with their very successful tri-electrode tube which is used in their GP4, GP5 and GP7 colour cameras.

In this system a striped filter is employed on the front of the vidicon but having three stripes of red, blue and green respectively. Instead of a conventional target disc a striped target is employed, with separate vertical stripes corresponding to the filter stripes. *Figure 3.7* shows how this appears in practice. As each target will only see either the red, green or blue parts of the scene then the three primary colours can be produced without any form of multiplexing. This gives a purer colour picture. The luminance component of the signal is derived by adding the green to the combined red and blue signals.

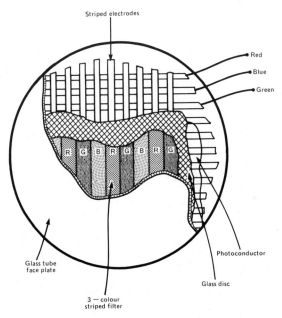

Figure 3.7. Diagram showing the construction of the face plate and target of the Hitachi tri-electrode vidicon tube, designed for single-tube colour cameras

A disadvantage of all these types of striped tube is that they do produce a very fine patterning on the screen as the signal is affected by the filter stripes. In general, this is only noticeable on thin vertical edges such as a title caption or a diagram, and appears as a slight zig-zagging and colour loss in the otherwise straight lines and really is a very small price to pay for otherwise very acceptable colour.

Component circuits

Although the vidicon tube has been described as the heart of the camera it needs many other components to function correctly. *Figure 3.8* shows the block diagram of a typical low-cost domestic black and white camera, in this case the JVC GS1000. When this is compared with *Figure 3.9* the block diagram of the Hitachi GP4 single-tube colour camera, it is apparent that both cameras have many features in common. Indeed, all the colour camera seems to have extra is three times as many circuits – one for each

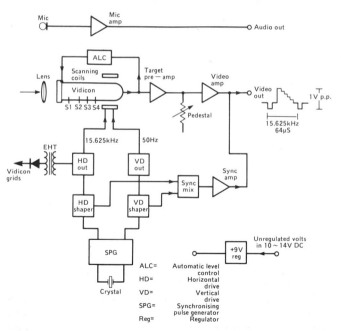

Figure 3.8. Block diagram of JVC GS1000 black and white camera

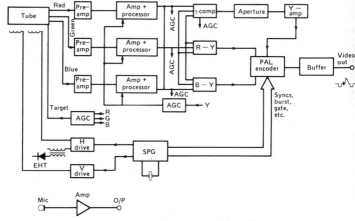

Figure 3.9. GP4 camera block diagram

colour channel! In fact this is generally true. All the principles of the black and white camera hold true for colour. Besides the tube, other major building blocks are the power supply, line and field synchronising circuits, signal processing and signal amplifying circuits.

Power supply

The design of the power supply will vary among different manufacturers and between cameras designed for different purposes. For example, a portable camera will have to run off batteries, whereas a studio camera, can have a mains power supply. Most domestic cameras run off 12 volts d.c. which is often supplied from a mains adaptor via a multicore cable. Some, such as the Hitachi GP7, can also be run off rechargeable batteries making them ideal for use with portable VTRs. The power supply circuitry has to cope with more than 12 volts however as the grids of the vidicon need up to 500 volts to function. So the power supply has to work in a similar manner to a television EHT circuit, with an inverter-type circuit.

Scanning

This is a process whereby the vidicon target is scanned by the electron beam, and this is achieved by similar means to those employed in a television receiver. Coils surrounding the tube deflect the beam by inducing magnetic fields. These coils, line and field, are fed with pulses from some type of synchronising pulse generator. This can be arranged to ensure that the normal 2 to 1 interlace of two fields to make one frame occurs.

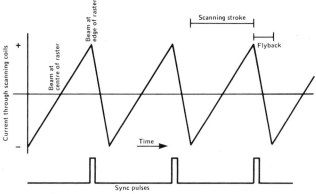

Figure 3.10. Diagram showing the relationships between the sync pulses and the current flowing through the vidicon scanning coils

Interlacing is done to ensure that the flicker rate of the picture is not distracting and doubles the picture repetition rate without a significant increase in signal bandwidth. This is most important for use in restricted broadcast frequencies. In the UK, a field frequency of 50 Hz is used along with a line frequency of 15.625 kHz. Therefore the frame frequency in the UK is 25 Hz. The field frequency of 50 Hz is useful on simple cameras as the mains in the UK is held to 50 Hz very precisely, so costly crystal controlled synchronising pulse generators can be avoided. The line drive pulses are more difficult to derive and often either crystals or inductance/capacitance oscillators are employed. The latter are really only suitable for the more simple type of camera. *Figure 3.10* shows some of the waveforms commonly associated with synchronising and scanning circuits.

Synchronising

Many domestic cameras have the synchronising generating circuits contained in the camera head and it is in this area where the
use of integrated circuits is prominently displayed. Many domestic cameras employ a single large-scale integrated circuit to
generate not only the line and field drive pulses but also the
various waveforms required for colour operation. Not long ago a
similar circuit would have occupied a 4 inch high by 19 inch wide
rack of equipment. The positioning of the synchronising pulse
generator (SPG) in the camera head does create a problem when
more than one camera is required, that is when synchronised
mixes, fades and cuts are needed. Although this rarely happens
in the domestic situation it is worth looking at the matter in a bit
more detail. To achieve, say, a gradual transition from the
picture viewed by camera one to that viewed by camera two it is
essential that the line and field drive circuits are absolutely in

*Figure 3.11. A Hitachi GP7 top end of the domestic market colour
cameras, ideal for low-cost industrial use (Ian Hirstle)*

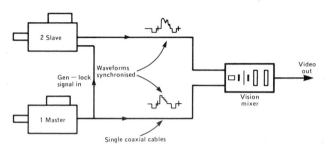

Figure 3.12. Diagram showing how two cameras such as Hitachi GP7s can be 'gen-locked' together to allow for mixes, fades, etc.

synchrony, otherwise one camera could be scanning on line 202 whilst the other was in the middle of the field flyback! A very unstable mix would result. In colour cameras it is essential that the colour subcarriers of each camera are also in phase or else colour shifts will occur. In studio cameras this is achieved by having a centralised SPG and feeding each camera with its required wave forms. This approach was also adopted by some of the earlier portable cameras such as the Sony Video Rover. Many of the domestic single-tube cameras cannot be used in multiple hookups, but those that can, for example the GP7 (*Figure 3.11*), have a system called 'Gen-locking,' whereby the camera's internal SPG is locked to an external video waveform. *Figure 3.12* shows two GP7s being used in a multiple-camera operation. This allows for single- or multiple-camera operations without any extra equipment.

Signal processing and amplifying circuits

Again these vary between black and white and colour and between different manufacturers but they are all designed to fulfil the same purpose. The current which emerges from the vidicon is very small and needs to be amplified very close to the vidicon tube. Often a low-noise FET (Field Effect Transistor) is employed for this purpose. The signal is now amplified further and any corrections applied. In a black and white camera these may consist of control of the black level (that is, the signal between the blackest part of the picture and the bottom of the blanking pulse) and gamma correction.

This latter is not to be confused with the film term of the same name but this is a measure of the linearity of response of any part of the camera system. For example a video amplifier is normally

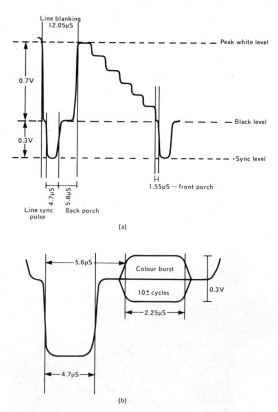

Figure 3.13. Video outputs. (a) Typical black and white video waveform as seen on an oscilloscope. (b) A colour signal is similar and has a colour burst in the back porch area

designed to give an output identical to the input; a grey scale fed in should emerge the same. Thus the amplifier can be said to have a gamma of one. A vidicon however has a gamma of around 0.5 to 0.7 and does not therefore have a linear response. Consequently a non-linear amplifier is needed to correct this. A colour camera will have the above circuits as well as colour-correcting ones. Finally, the output amplifier will mix the processed vidicon signal with the sync pulses to produce a standard video output (*Figure 3.13*). Often a sample of this signal will be tapped-off to feed an electronic viewfinder on top of the camera. This can be very useful not only as an aid to framing shots correctly but also as an 'instant replay' facility when the camera is used with a portable VTR.

Some of the features commonly found on domestic cameras and points to consider when buying and using one will now be explained.

Typical cameras

A typical black and white and a typical colour camera are shown in *Figures 3.14* and *3.15,* and although aimed at different price

Figure 3.14. JVC GS 1000 low-cost black and white camera (Ian Hirstle)

Figure 3.15. JVC GX88 lightweight colour camera (JVC)

ranges they have much in common. Both are similar in size, weight and operational complexity to a Super 8 cine camera. Almost all the controls are totally automatic.

Black and white

The JVC GS1000 has only four user controls. These are: the trigger to start and stop the video tape recorder when the camera is used with one, a manual open and close lever to cap and uncap the vidicon tube, a three-position lens iris and a very simple two-times zoom lens. There are no lens focus or other adjustments. This camera has an optical viewfinder which in this case works through the lens, so that you can see what the camera is 'looking at.' It also has a microphone built into the front of it, as do most domestic cameras. This ensures that sound is recorded on the video tape along with the picture, but it can also pick up the cameraman's breathing and lens movement noises. To use the camera is simplicity itself; all one does is point and shoot! The lens can be set wide open for indoor use or closed down slightly for shooting outside. The vidicon auto target circuit gives precisely the correct exposure.

Colour

The GP4 (*Figure 3.16*) is a bit more complicated, as one would expect with a colour camera. Again it has a trigger for use with a

Figure 3.16. Hitachi GP4 low-cost colour camera (Ian Hirstle)

VTR and also a built-in microphone. The zoom lens is more complex with focus, iris and zoom controls. There are only two other user controls however; one to increase the camera's gain for use in low lighting and the other to adjust the colour balance to match the camera so that it may work in any type of illumination. The problem of colour balance is an interesting one and is related to the colour temperature of the source of light illuminating an object. Those familiar with colour slide films will know that there are different types of film for use in daylight and artificial light. If the wrong type of film is used the resulting photo is either too blue or too red. It is exactly the same with colour television cameras. The human eye and brain will say that a green apple is green under almost any lighting conditions but a camera cannot do this. It sees the colour of the object due to the light it reflects from the illuminating source, and if lit with a blue light the apple will appear quite blue.

There are two ways a camera can be made to cope with this. One, as in still photography, is to use a filter over the lens and the other is electronically to tailor the vidicon's output to the lighting conditions. The former approach is usually found in broadcast cameras while the latter is more frequently encountered on domestic ones. The colour temperature control on the GP4 allows it to be matched for any lighting from studio floodlights, though mid-day sunlight, to overcast weather. This is achieved by altering the gains of the red and blue channels and keeping the green gain constant. A meter on the camera side shows the blue/red balance and can be set to the centre null position whilst 'shooting' a white card or wall, etc. Having set the balance correctly, all other colours should be rendered satisfactorily.

Second-generation colour cameras

The GP4 camera is capable of giving quite adequate pictures, but is essentially a 'no frills' model, as is reflected in its very reasonable price. A recent trend in domestic video equipment has been to develop a range of more sophisticated models, aimed at the user who demands more facilities from his equipment and is prepared to pay the correspondingly higher price. This trend first became apparent with various VTRs, such as the JVC HR 7700 and the Sony C7.

Sony have also introduced a second generation camera, the HVC 2000P (*Figure 3.17*). The approximate selling price of this

Figure 3.17. Sony HVC 2000P. A more sophisticated colour camera, with a number of second generation features (Ian Hirstle)

camera is £590, for which a buyer not only gets a very acceptable colour picture but also a host of other features which help to make home video productions more professional. One of the most obvious of these is the supplied electric zoom, auto iris lens, which also has a macro facility. This latter, coupled with the camera's ability to give acceptable colour pictures under low lighting conditions, makes it well suited to shooting flat copy, plants, small animals and pet fish, etc. The supplied electronic

view-finder makes framing shots easy and also allows instant
playback of tapes on location. Besides the normal 'low battery'
and 'tape running' indicators, three other indicators in the
viewfinder show lens aperture, colour temperature and video
waveform. A built-in microphone is standard, and a small LED
on the camera rear flashes to indicate that sound is being picked
up. Another interesting feature is a fader control, which allows
shots to be faded in and out along with the video tape starting
and stopping. This helps to make the disturbances between
various 'takes' less noticeable.

The camera can also be operated at a distance by an optional
remote control unit, which can be used with the camera's
detachable electronic viewfinder. In this way the camera may be
positioned in a hazardous area or in an inaccessible position and
controlled from a distance whilst the picture is monitored in the
viewfinder.

With all these features, this camera truly points the way in
which domestic video products are heading.

Zoom lenses

Most domestic cameras have some type of zoom lens fitted even
if it is only a two-times one as on the GS1000. These lenses are
very useful as they allow you to fill the screen with the object of
attention without having to move the position of the camera.
This can be very helpful, as after a wide-angle establishing shot
you can move to a close-up merely by zooming the lens. Be
careful though; do not use the zoom lens for the sake of it as this
again can distract from the value of the picture, Most domestic
cameras available today are capable of giving quite acceptable
black and white or colour pictures at very reasonable prices.
However, a few tips are in order to ensure that the best possible
results are obtained. Although intended for hand-held use most
cameras have a tripod or monopod socket on them somewhere
which is well worth using (*Figure 3.18*). It is very difficult and
tiring to hold the camera steady for more than about thirty

Figure 3.18. Second generation VHS portable recorder and colour camera, showing the use of a tripod (camera, 3V02; recorder, 3V24) (Thorn)

seconds and a swaying picture will not be very watchable on playback.

Lighting

The automatic light-level controls fitted in most cameras can be very useful but they can also be a nuisance if no override switch is fitted. For example, if shooting outdoors and recording a scene into the sun then the automatic level control (ALC) measures the average light intensity and reduces the tube sensitivity accordingly. This means that the person in the foreground will be very dark and the sky just about correctly exposed! The only solution is to shoot with the sun behind you. The same problem can occur indoors with a window behind your subject. The answer is either to shoot with the light behind you, that is move the subject, or to shut the curtains and use artificial light. To achieve successful lighting is not easy. The best that one can hope to achieve in the home is to lift the light levels up to the 700/1000 lux required to give reasonable colour with most cameras. The easiest way to do this is with a floodlight of the type sold for Super 8 movies; a one kilowatt light will be adequate for most applications.

Specialist cameras

The conventional vidicon tube will give quite reasonable black and white pictures in lighting levels as low as 50 lux and will give some sort of signal in levels of around 5 lux. 50 lux is the sort of light level found in a domestic sitting room in the evening with average house lights on. For security applications it is desirable to be able to get pictures in lighting conditions far worse than these, so a different type of tube is needed. A nuvicon tube is very similar to a vidicon but is more sensitive and gives useful pictures at around 1 lux. To work at levels lower than this, say around 0.5 lux, then a silicon target vidicon can be employed.

In these tubes the antimony trisulphide target of the vidicon is replaced by an array of silicon photodiodes with which conventional beam scanning can be used. The tube output resulting from a particular level of light is much greater than in normal tube, and the 'siticon' is very resistant to *lag* and *burn-in*. These are two problems to which vidicons are always prone. Lag is a phenomenon which occurs if the camera is pointed at an object for several minutes and then moved, the image of the object remaining on the tube for several seconds afterwards. This is particularly obvious at low light levels or when a bright image, say a candle flame, moves across the scene. This is often called 'comet tailing.' An extension of the same problem occurs when a camera is pointed at a bright light (either artificial or the sun). This results in nasty black spots or lines being 'burned' into the target. If you are lucky they can be removed by pointing the camera at a bright, white, defocused object, such as a white wall. If you are unlucky, then the tube will have to be replaced which for GP4 may cost about £150. For even lower light levels than this there is a choice between a camera fitted with a silicon intensifier target (SIT) or an intensified silicon intensifier target (ISIT)! The former will work down to 3.5×10^{-3} lux; that is moonlight, and the latter down to an incredible 3×10^{-4} lux – rather poor starlight! The price of around £6000 puts the ISIT camera firmly into the military/professional security market, however.

CCD cameras – the future?

A final interesting development is the CCD (Charge Coupled Device) camera. Although only in the experimental/specialist phase as yet, the CCD camera offers the possibilities of a true solid-state camera. In these the vidicon tube is replaced by an array of semi-conductors similar to silicon photodiodes. As an average 1 inch diameter vidicon is 8 inches long the fact that a CCD array of 150×120 elements is only 6 millimetres square by 2 millimetres deep represents quite a space saving. GEC, RCA and Fairchild are just three companies with stakes in the CCD field – Fairchild having an experimental broadcast quality 448×380 element array on a 10×12 millimetre chip. Although CCDs are immune to shock, magnetic fields and burn-in, and have a long life, they are very prone to image blooming and need complex circuitry to interface them with normal television circuits.

CCD cameras, complete with a miniature VTR in the camera head have been demonstrated by Sony and Hitachi, while the former have also demonstrated a very small solid-state pickup camera and the latter are now marketing the KP 500. This all-solid-state camera is very interesting and employs a three-plate metal oxide semiconductor (MOS) device in place of the vidicon tube. Like CCD cameras this system has high sensitivity

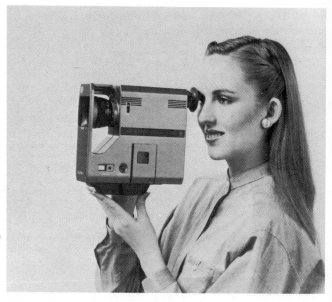

Figure 3.19. Sony experimental 'Video Movie' combined colour camera and VTR (Sony)

and features no 'sticking' (or excessive retention of image), no comet tailing, no geometric distortion and has a high immunity to external magnetic fields. A vertical resolution of 350 lines is possible.

It has been confidently predicted that within ten years combined CCD camera/recorder units will be commonplace and may well have relegated the Super 8 cine camera into a museum piece.

4 Video tape recorders

A video tape recorder is a machine for recording television pictures on magnetic tape, just as an audio tape recorder records sounds on tape. In this chapter, first the history and development of video tape recorders will be discussed – primarily in the domestic field but also with reference to the professional area from which these machines developed. Then a look at some technical principles and how some of the problems have been overcome will be followed by a speculative view of the future of domestic video tape recorders.

History

First of all, a brief digression on nomenclature. The term *video tape recorder* is usually abbreviated to 'VTR'. Strictly speaking this can be applied to all types of video recorders, whether using open reel-to-reel tapes or various cassette formats. However, since the large-scale introduction of cassette video recorders onto the domestic market the term 'video cassette recorder' has been coined. It is quite common to see this abbreviated to 'VCR' – which is, unfortunately, a Philips trade mark for their N1500 video machine cassette format. Throughout this chapter the term 'VTR' is used to indicate any type of video recorder, whether using open reels or cassettes. 'VCR' is thus correctly reserved for use in describing the Philips format.

The drive to produce a practical VTR came from the broadcast television companies in the USA. With a five-hour west to east time-zone difference across the USA, any form of national television programme had to be stored somehow for transmission at the appropriate time of the day for the different regions. Most television shows were live, with 16mm film being used to 'tele-record' any required programmes. A special 16mm film camera coupled to modified television monitor recorded the programmes, which when processed could be transmitted using a telecine machine. The problems with the system were that the picture quality was not very good and the costs were rather high.

Experimentation with modified designs of magnetic tape recorders for recording television pictures had been going on since the early 1950s. The main patent for two-headed helical scan VTRs (the basis for all current domestic VTRs) was filed by Telefunken in 1953. At the same time Toshiba in Japan were experimenting with very basic helical-scan VTRs, whilst RCA in the United States demonstrated a fixed-head longitudinal-scan VTR.

Quadruplex

The first functional VTR was demonstrated by Ginsburg, Anderson and Dolby (yes, the same man) of Ampex in October 1956 at the SMPTE's convention in Los Angeles. This machine used two-inch video tape drawn past vertically rotating video heads. The format was called 'quadruplex' as it employed four video heads. The format rapidly became an industrial standard for broadcasters throughout the world, as it still is today.

Work on different techniques for designing VTRs continued and in 1958 the BBC demonstrated VERA (Video Electronic Recording Apparatus), a longitudinal-scan fixed head video tape recorder. This, like the RCA machine in the States relied on drawing video tape, very rapidly, past stationary recording heads. Although it worked, it was dropped in favour of quadruplex VTRs. Further refinements and improvements occurred throughout the late 1950s and early 1960s with Sony producing its CV2000 half-inch helical-scan transistorised VTR for the industrial market in 1965. This was essentially a non-broadcast machine, and in fact the CV in the title stood for Consumer Video. This very practical and hardworking VTR appeared on the UK market as a 405 line machine and was replaced by the improved CV2100 in 1968 – a 625/405 line compatible VTR.

Various other manufacturers, including Matsushita (Panasonic) and Shibaden (Hitachi) introduced similar black and white VTRs in the late 1960s and early 1970s, most being based around open-reel half-inch tape, although Ikigami chose two-thirds of an inch tape for some of their VTRs. All these machines were designed for the industrial non-broadcast market and found very little use as domestic-use VTRs. No timer or off-air tuner was incorporated and the styling was definitely utility. A degree of standardisation for industrial VTRs was brought about by the EIAJ (Electronic Industries Association of Japan) who agreed on a half-inch monochrome and colour standard to be implemented by all the Japanese electronic manufacturers. This allowed tapes recorded on, say, a Sony CV3620 to be played back on a National NV3030.

It is to be regretted that this degree of cooperation and standardisation has not been carried forward to the current generation of domestic video cassette recorders. 1969 saw the demonstration of what was probably the first domestic VTR using cassettes rather than open reel-to-reel tapes. This machine, based on the colour EIAJ tape format, was produced in limited quantities by Ampex in the United States. In 1970 Sony demonstrated their sophisticated three-quarter inch U-matic VTR, selling it in Japan and the States the following year and in the UK in 1972. Over ten different manufacturers adopted the U-matic format and this has rapidly become an unofficial industrial standard, not only in Japan and the USA, but also in Europe. The introduction of editing VTRs and portable battery-operated U-matics in 1975 helped consolidate the format's position as did the introduction of the triple-standard VO2630 U-matic in 1978. This allowed, for the first time, the easy interchange of programmes recorded on any of the world's three television systems. As with the CV2100 VTR a few U-matics found their way into domestic use – often in the homes of professional television staff. No timer or tuner was included, so again it was not really suitable for domestic use.

The world's first true domestic VTR was announced in 1970 and first marketed in the UK in 1972. This was the cassette-loading Philips VCR, model type N1500. It incorporated an off-air TV tuner, RF modulator and basic timer and allowed a conventional television, either black and white or colour to be used with a VTR. With its cassette tape format and piano key type controls it was designed for ease of use by non-technical people and the relatively attractive styling ensured that the Philips VTR soon found its place in some better-off homes as well as in industry and education. Although its initial selling price of £325 was allegedly subsidised by the manufacturer, it was still a lot of money for domestic customers to spend when 99.9 per cent of them had never heard of a VTR and were unaware of what it could do for them.

Philips (and some of the other companies who adopted the format, such as Grundig, Pye and Skantic) launched a vast advertising campaign, explaining that the VCR would enable you to record one programme while watching another, to record a programme whilst you were out (using the built-in tuner and timer) and to record a television programme while your own TV set was switched off. Although pre-recorded software was not initially available, soon manufacturers started, in a small way, to fill this gap. Essentially the VTR sold on its ability to 'time-shift' broadcast programmes for viewing at a more convenient time. The current generation of VCRs have become far more sophisti-cated than the Philips N1500 but do exactly the same basic task.

Although Philips revised and improved the design of the N1500, through the N1501 to the N1502, the dual-concentric format of the video cassette used continued to cause mechanical problems. The 60 minutes playing time also, unfortunately, excluded the domestic use of the VCR to make unattended recordings of movies, football matches and other sporting e-vents. In 1976 a modified version of the VCR format appeared. Known as VCR-LP, it was a long-playing machine running at almost half the speed of the N1500 and so giving around two hours' recording. This machine, the N1700 and the slightly improved N1702, were subsequently revealed to have been intended as purely stop-gap machines, while the VCC (Video Compact Cassette) was designed and developed. The main need for such a stop-gap was that while Philips had the UK and European domestic markets to themselves from 1972 to 1975, the Japanese had not been idle.

Sony's Betamax one-hour domestic VTR appeared in the USA in 1975, employing a cassette with half-inch tape, but of a different design from that used by Philips. The Betamax VTR also had an off-air tuner, RF modulator and timer and was smaller and neater than the Philips VCR. When it and the rival (incompatible, but otherwise very similar) VHS (Video Home System) VTR from the Matsushita Corporation of Japan were introduced into the UK in 1978, they had all the above features as well as giving slightly over three hours' playing time – long enough for most movies and sports fixtures to be recoded. 1978 also saw the third derivation of the Philips VCR, the Grundig SVR (Super Video Recorder). This VTR made very little impression on the UK, although its sales in Europe were appreciable. A playing time of four hours from a cassette containing as much tape as gave one hour's recording on the original Philips' VCR was made possible by reducing tape speed yet again. By this point quality was noticeably worse than that given on the VCR, but was still acceptable for general domestic use. Solenoid operation and a digital timer capable of being set to make recordings up to ten days in advance were coupled to a digital self-seeking television tuner and station memory, making the VTR quite a sophisticated machine.

The first Betamax and VHS portable VTRs were introduced in 1979, the same year that some of the second generation of domestic VTRs appeared. Second generation means VTRs incorporating a whole host of features not found in machines in the past. The first improvement was seen in the incorporation of a digital timer capable of making a recording a week in advance of the setting date. This was followed by timers which could make several recordings at the same time of day on consecutive days; ideal for recording episodes of daily serials when you are on holiday. The logical conclusion of timer development now appears to have been reached, with the ability to make several recordings on different channels on different days, programmable up to a week or more in advance.

Having exhausted the possibilities of timers, the manufacturers turned their attention to what might be called various 'trick play' features. These include the ability to display a still picture, pictures in various rates of slow motion and fast motion, as well as frame by frame advance, etc. The value of these features does seem a little uncertain to most domestic users, although for sports training or industrial motion analysis they are undoubtedly of use. Infra-red remote control has also been applied to VTRs, allowing all the functions to be controlled from an armchair! Dolby noise reduction circuitry has recently been appearing in some domestic VTRs and limited forms of editing are also becoming commonplace. On the American market, always a good indicator of future UK video trends, fully automatic video tape editing units for Betamax format tapes have been available from Sony since 1978, and 1980 saw the introduction of a basic VHS editing suite from National in the UK. The large number of additional features appearing on domestic VTRs appear to make some of them so complex that 'technofear' may become apparent in some prospective purchasers!

Toshiba announced their prototype LVR (Longitudinal Video Tape Recorder) in 1979, which, with its low mechanical parts count, promised a considerable reduction in cost. BASF had first announced their (incompatible) longitudinal video tape recorder in 1974, but now they demonstrated a working prototype in the same year. Philips and Grundig announced their VCC, proudly proclaiming that it would be the European video format for the 1980s. This machine was revolutionary in that it employed a flip-over cassette which could be played on one side to the end and then turned over and played again, in the manner of that other great success of Philips, the compact audio cassette. The system called DTF (Dynamic Track Following) is also used to help ensure compatibility between different machines. The basic idea for this was adapted from broadcast technology. PAL versions of the VTR appeared in the UK at demonstrations in

1979 but it was the strangely-named Grundig '2×4' (the maximum playing time is twice 4 hours) which actually appeared first in British shops in the summer of 1980. VCC has reduced the cost of recording an hour of television programmes from £22 at 1972 prices to around £2.50 at 1980 prices. Several other European manufacturers have agreed to produce machines to this format but it remains to be seen if it can displace the well-established foothold of the Japanese. The odds appear to be against it.

Some current and recent domestic VTRs

Philips

Although obsolete, the Philips N1500, the first true domestic video recorder, is still around in quite large numbers (*Figure 4.1*). In fact, 35000 of them were sold in the UK between 1972 and 1978. Considerable thought had been given to making the

Figure 4.1. Philips domestic black and white camera and N1500 VTR (Philips)

machine 'consumer-proof', with only the sound level being available under optional manual control. A meter was provided to indicate the video input level, audio level and tracking level on playback, and a manual colour-killer was also provided. No

Figure 4.2. Philips N1520, an editing VTR to the Philips 1 hour VCR format (Ian Hirstle)

video input or outputs were provided as playback into a conventional TV set was the normal mode of use. Later versions of the N1500, such as the N1500M and the N1512 did, however, have these facilities.

Japanese VTRs

The first of the Japanese domestic VTRs to appear in the UK, the JVC HR3300, was much smaller and neater than the Philips' VCR and did not have the manual gain controls and the meter of the Philips. A digital timer enabled much more accurate recordings to be made. Interestingly, the JVC HR3300 appeared with a number of different 'makers' names on it, including Akai, Ferguson, Baird, Multibroadcast, DER and Granada. This

*Figure 4.3. A low-cost non-programmable VTR from Thorn,
the 3V22 (Thorn)*

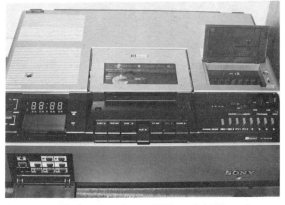

*Figure 4.4. The first Beta format VTR on the UK market was
this Sony SL 8000 (Closed Circuit Consultants)*

example of 'badge-engineering,' so common in the motor car
industry, has misled many people into thinking that some of
these VTRs are made in the UK, whereas in fact they are all
Japanese. Video inputs and outputs are provided as standard, so

these VTRs can be used with high-quality monitors as well as with conventional television sets. The Sony Betamax SL8000UB (*Figure 4.4*) offered almost identical features at a similar price, but using the incompatible Betamax cassette.

Figure 4.5. JVC HR 3660. A typical first-generation VTR, with a simple wired remote control (JVC)

The JVC HR3660 (*Figure 4.5*) was the first cassette-loading VTR to offer a form of wired remote control as well as a range of slow, fast and still play features. It also has an eight-day timer, but cannot be programmed to make recordings on more than one channel. A particularly interesting feature is the ability to give intelligible sound even when running at twice normal speed playback.

Another VHS machine, at the time of writing not available in the UK, is the HR6700. This incorporates most of the features of the HR3600 but has a fully programmable timer, enabling up to six programmes on six channels to be recorded at six times. It also has two recording speeds, giving in the USA two or six hours recording capacity. If this was introduced to the UK recording times would be three and eight hours – with reduced quality being the penalty for increased playing time. In fact many current US machines have three recording and playback speeds; SP (standard play), LP (long play), and SLP (super long play), the slowest speed giving the longest playing time – six hours. Multi-speed versions of Sony Betamax machines are also available in the States giving a maximum playing time of five hours. This, understandably is a source of considerable confusion.

It was a Beta format VTR from Sony, the SL8080, which first gave the solution to finding different programmes recorded on tape in one's absence. When the timer triggers and the recorder starts, a special pulse is recorded on the control track. When the VTR is later put into fast forward or rewind it automatically stops when a pulse is detected. This makes it easy to locate programmes on the tape, and to skip them as required. Sony, Mitsubishi, Sharp and JVC have all brought out machines of this type, of which the Sony C7 (*Figure 4.6*) was the first to incorporate a fully programmable timer. This quite elegant VTR comes complete with an infra-red remote control pad, which allows all the

Figure 4.6. The C7 second-generation VTR from Sony, designed to the Beta format (Sony)

functions to be controlled from an armchair. The timer is very sophisticated, allowing up to four programmes to be recorded over a 14-day period on up to four channels. A rapid search facility allows a three-hour tape to be reviewed in 16 minutes, which coupled with a tone-pulse programme-labelling system (as for the Sony SL8080 Betamax), makes finding a specific piece of material very easy. A range of slow motion and still facilities are provided as well. An interesting feature which had, until the C7,

Figure 4.7. The Sanyo VTC 9300 was the first domestic VTR to employ a microprocessor (Sanyo)

been confined to the professional market, was a simple type of editing control. This allows segments of television (either off-air or from a camera) to be joined almost imperceptibly.

VHS

Sony were the first to introduce a second-generation VTR, but they did not have the field to themselves for very long. Sharp, not a firm renowned for their involvement in video, introduced the VC6300, a VHS format VTR. With a range of features very similar to the C7, this has wired remote control and the ability to record up to seven programmes on seven days. A similar model, but with infra-red remote control appeared in 1981.

Figure 4.8. The Mitsubishi HS300 was one of the first VHS machines to offer a remote control facility (Mitsubishi)

Figure 4.9. JVC's top-of-the-range HR 7700 has all the features one could possibly want, including full infra-red remote control (JVC)

JVC's HR7700 (*Figure 4.9*) is a front-loading VHS machine, again with all the features of the rival VTRs. Interestingly, it is designed to accommodate the latest generation of very thin, long-playing-time VHS cassettes, giving 6½ hours playing time in total. Dolby noise reduction is also used to improve the sound quality.

Philips VCC

VHS and Betamax do not have the UK domestic VTR market entirely to themselves, even though the Philips N1500 and N1700 formats are obsolete. The new Video 2000 format from Philips is represented by Grundig's 2×4 and Philips own VR2020 VTRs (*Figure 4.10*). Both these machines use double-sided compact

Figure 4.10. Philips VR2020 Video 2000 format VTR (Philips)

video cassettes, giving up to eight hours' recording and have facilities for full remote control. A sophisticated timer allows several recordings on different channels to be made over several days.

Portable VTRs

These machines are designed for battery-operated use in the field with portable black and white or colour video cameras. Several of them can also be equipped with mains-operated television tuners and timers to enable them to double as home

Figure 4.11. The JVC HR4100 VTR was the first portable battery-operated VHS machine in the UK (JVC)

VTRs as well. The basic requirements of a portable VTR are that it must be relatively light, battery operated and robust. Although Akai produced some colour and black and white portable VTRs using quarter inch tape in the mid 1970s it was left to the JVC HR4100 VHS machine (*Figure 4.11*) to be the first genuine domestic portable VTR.

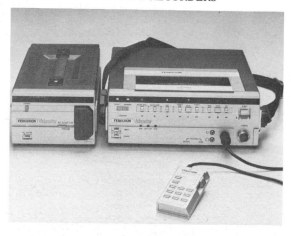

Figure 4.12. In contrast to Figure 4.11 the Thorn 3V34/3V26 VHS recorder and battery charger is the latest portable unit. It has a wired remote control and a range of special features (Thorn)

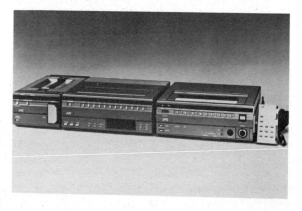

Figure 4.13. With this JVC HR2200 an optional tuner/timer unit enables the portable VTR to be used as a fully-programmable unit (JVC)

Using standard VHS format cassettes, this first-generation portable colour recorder could be used with a range of cameras, giving up to 30 minutes of recording from a built-in rechargeable battery. An optional plug-on timer and tuner unit allowed the HR4100 to be used as a mains-operated time-shifting VTR. Its associated mains power unit doubled as a battery charger. Weighing almost 10 kg and lacking the features of second-generation mains VTRs it was not surprising that it was replaced by the HR2200 VHS portable (*Figure 4.13*).

It is available as a badge-engineered design from Thorn as the 3V23. This very neat portable weighs around 5 kg, half the

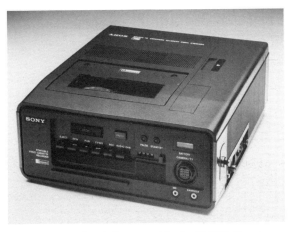

Figure 4.14. Sony's Beta portable, the SL3000 (Sony)

weight of the HR4100, and it has a wired remote control, fast picture search, reverse, still, etc. An auto-edit facility like that used on the Sony C7 and JVC's 7700 is employed to give clean transition between camera takes.

Sony were a bit slow off the mark in introducing a Betamax portable set to the UK, but the SL3000, on sale in late 1980, rectified this gap and it incorporated a range of second-generation features, including 'clean-cut editing' (*Figure 4.14*).

Advanced VTRs

There will always be a small, but specific demand for specialist
video facilities either from industry or wealthy individuals with
problems which are not solved by normal domestic VTRs.
Leaving aside the professional market (including industrial and
broadcast) let us look at some of the domestic VTRs that are
being produced to fill specialist niches.

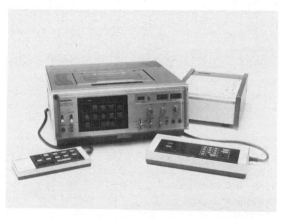

Figure 4.15. The National NV 8200 VHS VTR was designed for
industrial use. It omitted a tuner/timer but allowed editing and
had Dolby noise reduction circuits (National)

One of these was produced by a small UK firm and was
designed to extend the facilities of a standard JVC 3300 VHS
VTR. The Microtune 2000 unit (*Figure 4.16*) is a microprocessor-controlled device which simply interfaces with the
VHS deck and enables it to record up to 15 programmes on
seven channels up to a week in advance. At £200 in addition to
the price of the VTR, it was quite expensive, but useful until the
second generation of VTRs became available.

Similar small scale modifications of VTRs are still being
carried out; for example, several firms will modify old Philips

Figure 4.16. An interesting device, the Microtune 2000 was designed as an add-on to a range of VHS VTRs. It gave the user second-generation features before the manufacturer's VTRs became available (Closed Circuit Consultants)

N1500 VTRs to N1700 format, as well as giving a playing time of over five hours, remote control, programmable timer, etc.

A large area of interest is that brought about by the various incompatible television standards which exist around the world. The reader will recall from Chapter 1 that the USA uses a colour television system called NTSC, with 60 fields per second and 525 lines per picture, compared with the PAL system common in the UK and parts of Europe, which uses 50 fields and 625 lines. SECAM, the French system, also uses 50 fields and 625 lines but with a different colour coding system. Consequently a video tape made in the USA will not playback in Europe, and vice versa. SECAM and PAL tapes can be interchangeable, but will playback in black and white only. This is a problem professional broadcasters have solved with very expensive standards' converters; feed PAL in one end and get NTSC out of the other – nice, but at a price! The industrial user is catered for by a range of Sony U-matic three-quarter inch cassette VTRs of which the VO2630 is typical. This VTR will record programmes in either PAL, NTSC or SECAM, and playback onto a suitable monitor.

This is achieved by using some clever electronics in the VTR and monitor to allow for either 525/60 or 625/50 (lines/fields) and a non-standard NTSC colour signal. This is expensive however around £2000 for a VTR and monitor. A cheaper solution is obviously required for domestic use, where, for example, families wish to send tapes to relatives in different countries.

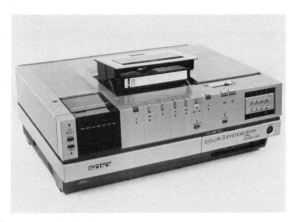

Figure 4.17. The Sony SLT-7ME can play back PAL, NTSC and SECAM video tapes (Sony)

Sony have produced a solution in the form of the SLT7ME, a Betamax format VTR similar to the C7, but capable of operating on a wide range of voltages and line frequencies and playing back PAL, NTSC and SECAM tapes (*Figure 4.17*). Sharp have a multi-standard version of their VC6300 and several small UK firms have produced modified VTRs suitable for multi-standard use, at a premium price however.

Technical aspects

Basically, a VTR does for a television signal what an audio recorder does for sound; that is, it enables the sound and vision components of the television signal to be recorded on magnetic tape. To record these signals, either a special television set is used, with sockets giving video and audio out or, more commonly in the domestic field, the VTR has its own built-in television tuner. Similarly, for playback, either a modified television set with video and audio facilities is needed which is expensive, or else the VTR must have a UHF modulator built-in. This device, a very low-powered television transmitter, combines the sound and vision signals from the VTR and presents them to the television aerial socket like a television signal, usually on channel 36. It is normal practice to rig the television aerial downlead through the VTR electronics and then to the television set, so that the television or recorder can be used independently. The TV set forms no part of the recording system so it can be left switched off.

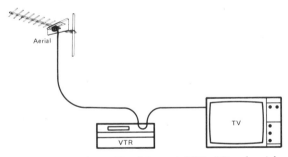

Figure 4.18. Relationship of domestic VTR, TV and aerial

As the recording process is not perfect, the pictures displayed on playback are not quite as good as the original off-air signals but the differences are very slight and represent a small price to pay for the convenience offered by a VTR.

Basic principles

All tape recorders work by laying down a track of residual magnetism in magnetic material deposited on the surface of the plastic tape. In other words, the random magnetic nature of the particles on a blank tape is modified in a predictable manner by a recording signal. This rearrangement of magnetism is read on playback and used to produce an output signal almost identical to the original. In all recorders a recording head, which consists of a metal core covered in a coil of wire, is used to effect this change and also to read the tape on playback (*Figure 4.19*). The magnetism flows through the metal of the head until it reaches the gap where a high-reluctance air gap forces the magnetism to flow through the particles on the tape, rearranging them. A good domestic audio tape recorder (reel-to-reel) can handle signals from 20 Hz to 20 kHz, as present day recording tapes have a

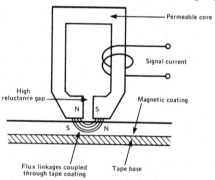

Figure 4.19. Magnetic tape recording – basic theory

dynamic range of around 70 dB. This is equivalent to around 10 octaves of bandwidth (an octave is the section frequency scale over which the frequency doubles; 10 to 20 Hz, 2 Hz to 4 Hz, etc. There are 6 octaves between 20 Hz and 1280 Hz). It is obvious from this that conventional audio recording techniques will not allow a full colour television signal, with a frequency range of 25 Hz to 5.5 MHz, to be recorded.

The solution to this is to use a FM (frequency modulation) system of recording as opposed to the familiar amplitude-modulated audio recorder. Not only does FM recording overcome the 10 octave barrier by reducing the octave range of the television signal, it also increases the signal to noise ratio by employing a fully saturated tape. Even so, a point occurs where the high-frequency limit of the tape is reached and the signal output drops to zero. This happens when the recorded wavelength approaches the size of gap in the magnetic head. Those readers familiar with audio recorders will know that the faster the tape speed, the better the recording of the higher frequencies. For example, if a 1 Hz signal is being recorded on a machine running at 15 inches per second, then the 1 Hz signal will occupy 15 inches of tape, and thus tape speed and signal frequency determine the length of the track occupied by a full signal cycle. As signal frequency increases, the recorded wavelength decreases. A 10 Hz signal at 15 inches per second occupies 1.5 inches, and so on. There are two solutions to this problem; the head gap can be made as small as possible (0.6 – 0.3µm are common on VTRs) and the other is to increase the speed at which the tape passes the video heads. Early experimental broadcast VTRs used massive spools of tape running up to 360 inches per second (14.17 m/s) past fixed recording heads. The problem with this approach was that over 20 miles of tape would be needed to give one hour's playing time! Interestingly enough, this longitudinal video recording technique has recently re-surfaced as potential domestic format. The answer was to move both the video heads *and* the tape so that a high effective tape-to-head, or writing, speed was obtained. The original Amplex video tape recorder, built to the four-head quadruplex format rotated the video heads across two-inch wide magnetic tape. An effective writing speed of 1500 inches per second (38.1 m/s) was used with the tape running at 15 inches per second. With a head gap of 0.6 µm, the shortest recorded wavelength must be 1.2µm, or in other words, twice the head gap. This ensures that the recorded signal is roughly linear with respect to frequency. If a bandwidth of 5.5 MHz is needed to record a full colour signal, then the required tape speed will be:

$$\text{speed (m/s)} = \text{wavelength (m)} \times \text{frequency (Hz)}$$
$$= (1.2 \times 10^{-6}) \times (5.5 \times 10^{6})$$
$$= 6.6 \text{ m/s}$$
$$\text{(or 259 inches per second)}$$

This can be compared with the effective writing speed of domestic VTRs (*Table 4.1*) for example, that for Betamax VTR is 6.6 m/s (259 inches per second) and that for VHS is 4.8 m/s (189 inches per second).

Helical scan

Having looked at some of the general theory behind magnetic recording and at the idea of using rotating video heads to achieve a high writing speed, we will now see how this theory is applied to some domestic VTRs.

The four-headed quadruplex format employing two-inch wide tape may be satisfactory for broadcast use but is not all suitable for domestic use as the electronics involved alone make the cost prohibitive. An alternative to using four heads is to use only one or two and to wrap the tape further around the rotating video heads. The principle is used in all current domestic and industrial VTRs. The tape is guided at an angle around the surface of a rotating head drum (which houses the video heads) so that the

Table 4.1. Comparison of videotape formats

Format	Tape width (mm)	Tape speed (cm/sec)	Video track pitch (µm)	Writing speed (m/sec)	Sound track width (mm)	Max playing time (hours)	Audio response (Hz)
VCR	12.7	14.29	130	8.10	0.7	1	120-12000
VHS	12.7	2.339	49	4.8	1.0	4	70-8000
Beta	12.7	1.873	32.8	6.6	1.05	3.6	50-8000
VCR-LP	12.7	6.56	85	8.1	0.7	3	120-10000
SVR	12.7	3.95	50	8.21	0.7	4.25	80-10000
V2000	12.7	2.44	22.6	5.08	0.325 (2 off)	8.00	–
BASF -LVR	8	4.00	–	4.0	–	–	40-12500
Toshiba -LVR	12.7	6.00	–	6.0	–	–	–

NB   All audio response figs to ±9dB

lanting path described by the heads across the tape is part of a helix – hence the term 'helical scan'. On reflection, you will realise that if the tape goes 180° around the drum then two heads need to be used, whereas if it goes 360° – all the way round – then only one head need be employed. This, however, causes problems as no signal is produced on playback during the time between the head leaving the tape and rejoining it. It is also mechanically difficult to produce a cassette-loading 360°-wrap, so for these two reasons, all domestic VTRs are two-headed, 180°-wrap helical scan machines.

In practice, the speed of head rotation is normally timed to enable one field ($312\frac{1}{2}$ lines) of picture to be recorded at each head pass. In other words with the head drum rotating at 25 rpm, two fields, occupying one-fiftieth of a second may be recorded during each revolution. Each video track thus contains a single field. The size of the head drum also comes into the calculation because writing speed is:

$$25 \times \pi \times \text{drum diameter}$$

So for the VHS system, writing speed is:

$$25 \times \pi \times 6.2 = 487 \text{ cm/s}$$

Thus as the head drum diameter decreases, all other things being equal, the writing speed decreases, so to keep the performance up a smaller drum must be linked with a faster linear tape speed.

Video Resolution			Video signal: noise (dB)	Cost per hour	Audio wow & flutter (%DIN)	Audio signal: noise (dB)
3MHz	colour	−26dB	≥40	£22	0.3	≥38
3.2MHz	mono					
3MHz	colour	−13dB	≥39	£4.83	0.3	≥42.5
3.3MHz	mono					
2.9MHz	colour	−10dB	≥40	£4.18	0.32	≥42
3.3MHz	mono					
3MHz	colour	−14dB	≥40	£6.18	0.25	≥44.5
3.3MHz	mono					
3MHz	colour	−6dB	≥39	£5.40	0.3	≥43
3.4MHz	mono					
–			–	£2.50	–	–
3MHz		−6dB	≥40	?	0.01%	≥56dB
–			–	–	–	–

Each pass of the video head records one complete field (1/5 second) on each pass so we shall now see how the heads are timed to arrive at the edge of the tape in time to start a new television field.

To solve this problem a servo system is employed which derives a master 25 Hz pulse from the field syncs of the incoming video.This is compared with a 25 Hz pulse produced by the rotating head drum, generated by a small permanent magnet attached to the drum which passes over a pick-up coil once every revolution. It is positioned so that the pulse is generated as one of the video heads is just about to pass across the tape. If the two pulses from the reference and the head drum are coincident, then all is well and both heads complete fields across the tape. If a mistiming occurs and a complete field is not recorded then the head drum pulse will be either early or late and the comparator will produce a d.c. control voltage to slow down or speed up the drum rotation so as to achieve coincidence. This dynamic control is monitored with each revolution of the head drum.

On playback it is no use locking the head rotation to the incoming video signal, as it will bear no timing relationship to the signal on the tape. Instead a control track of 25 Hz pulses, laid down on the tape during recording and derived from the field sync on the recorded video, is used and the head drum is locked to the control track pulses. Thus again, the video heads play back a whole television field on each pass.

Tape format

Having described how the video heads put tracks of information onto the tape we will now consider how these physically appear on the tape. *Figure 4.20* shows how the Philips VCR cassette VTR lays its tracks down. Video tracks are recorded at an angle as the tape runs past the heads on a slope – helical scan. A control track is recorded by a fixed head using standard audio recorder techniques. The audio track, at the top of the tape is also recorded by a fixed head, usually in the same assembly as

he control track head, again using standard audio recorder
echniques. The blank spaces, guard tracks, are provided to
eparate the video, control and audio tracks and to prevent
ross-talk between signals.

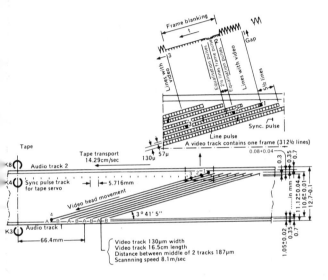

Figure 4.20. Philips VCR track format

One problem with the guard tracks between the video tracks is
that they reduce the amount of tape available for recording
information. With modern domestic VTRs, where playing time
and hence a low cost per hour is at a premium, it is essential to
pack information onto the tape as densely as possible. This is
achieved by doing away with the guard track between video
tracks and employing a technique called *slant azimuth recording*
to reduce the intolerable cross-talk which would otherwise
occur. This would be particularly noticeable where the video
heads might scan adjacent, irrelevant tracks and so produce a
noisy, distorted picture. In other words, the video heads have to

track correctly and usually a customer control is provided to optimise this adjustment, which is particularly useful for playing back recordings made on another VTR.

Slant azimuth recording

The only way to get track isolation without using guard tracks is to ensure that, for example, video head A only reads on playback video tracks initially recorded by head A, and similarly for head B. Those readers familiar with audio recorders will know that when a playback head azimuth adjustment, (that is, the adjustment in relationship to the horizontal) is incorrect, the recording will be replayed but without the high frequency end of the signal (*Figure 4.21*). It is this principle which is applied to current domestic VTRs. Video heads are tilted, ±15° in the Philips VCR-LP format, so that a total tilt of 30° is provided between the two heads. This ensures that, for example, if head A reads some of head B's video track the information will be 30° out of phase and so not played back, (or to be precise, it will be detected, but at a very low level). This effectively means that the high frequency end, (greater than 1.5 MHz) of irrelevant tracks will not be misread by the heads. The effect of the low frequency

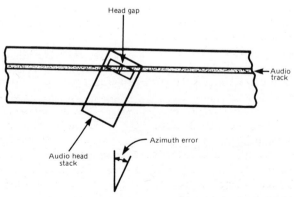

Figure 4.21. Azimuth error (exaggerated)

end of the signal, which does appear as cross-talk, is removed by sophisticated filters and will be discussed in the section on colour processing.

Colour recording systems

The FM recording system previously described allows the full colour signal, with a bandwidth of 5.5 MHz to be recorded on broadcast or superior industrial VTRs. Unfortunately it is not possible to achieve this on domestic VTRs, or indeed most industrial ones, as bandwidth limitations and timebase errors introduce problems. Bandwidth problems arise as a domestic VTR does not have a high enough writing speed to encode a full signal, due to the small size of the video head drum. Although this could be enlarged a very cumbersome VTR would result. The timebase error problem is essentially due to mechanical inertia and tolerance in the VTR. This has the effect of disturbing the way the sync signals are laid down and consequently gives a distorted picture or false colour on playback.

The solution to this problem is to use a system which allows the timebase inadequacies to be hidden and is called heterodyne or colour-under processing. The term heterodyne refers to the mixing together of two signals of different frequency to produce a third or yet another frequency. In all domestic VTRs the high frequency colour signal is shifted from around 4.43 MHz to around 600-700 kHz and directly recorded in the area that would otherwise by occupied by the lower FM luminance sideband. This reduces the luminance resolution but only to very small extent. As the filtered-out colour signal is recorded at a frequency below that used for the luminance it is called a *colour-under* system (*Figure 4.22*). In VHS recorders the colour carrier frequency of 627 kHz is employed while 687 kHz is used in Beta format recorders. These figures are arrived at by filtering the chroma information out from the luminance and mixing it (hetrodyning) with a further signal from a stable oscillator. In VHS recorders this is 5.06 MHz giving a difference signal of 627 kHz, and in Beta recorders 5.1 MHz, giving around 687 kHz as the new carrier frequency.

These carrier signals are mixed with the FM luminance signal and are not themselves frequency modulated. In other words they are amplitude modulated signals relying upon the luminance FM signal to supply the high frequency bias signal which is required in ordinary audio recorders.

On playback, essentially the reverse system is used to recover the low frequency colour signal then multiply it back up in frequency to around 4.43 MHz. It can then be combined with the luminance information and supplied as a normal PAL signal.

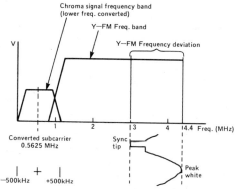

Figure 4.22. Colour-under and relationship to FM sidebands

Because the local oscillator is highly stable, it enables variations in tape speed and tape stretching to be evened out and a reasonable colour fidelity to be maintained. Also, as no colour decoding/encoding takes place, phase errors resulting in incorrect colours are most unlikely to occur.

Readers will recall that the use of slanted video heads to allow higher densities of information to be packed onto the tape rely on the high frequency end of the video signal being rapidly attenuated by the azimuth differences between heads. Unfortunately, the effects of azimuth alignment are very small on the low frequency (600 – 700 kHz) colour signal and chroma cross-talk becomes a considerable problem. Sophisticated devices called comb filters are employed to reduce this low frequency cross-talk and they can be considered as a form of delay line. Although there are differences in design between VHS and Beta VTRs, the principle is the same and relies on a chroma signal being divided in two, with half being passed through a delay line and half bypassing it. When the direct and delayed signals are added together, the desired in-phase components are added and the unwanted, out-of-phase, cross-talk signals are subtracted, hence reducing the level of chroma cross-talk. This results in high fidelity colour production.

Drop-out compensators (DOCs)

These interesting circuits are never given much thought until they go wrong. Their function is to supply an output signal where none exists! Modern tapes are made to a very high quality, but even so, they suffer from what is termed drop-out. This is where the magnetic oxide has become damaged in some way, so that it can no longer retain a signal. Where this happens noise will appear in the picture, which, especially on used or second-hand tapes, can become quite considerable. The drop-out compensator helps to alleviate this problem by filling the gap in the picture with the information from a previous television line. In effect a drop-out compensator consists of a 64μs (one horizontal line) delay line and the switching/sensing circuit (*Figure 4.23*). The output from the 1 H delay line is not normally used, but when

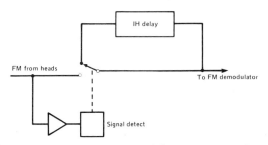

Figure 4.23. Block diagram of drop-out compensator (DOC)

the signal level drops below a pre-set value (which will occur in the case of a drop-out) the output from the delay line is switched-in to give a signal. Although only 64μs (or 1 line) long, drop-outs of several times this length may be hidden by using the same replacement line repeated several times.

Conventional PAL theory would indicate that having two or more adjacent lines all with the same colour-burst phase-relationship would cause chroma problems with the picture. In practice the colour problems are very small and it is not considered worthwhile to use a 2 H delay line which would be required to maintain the correct PAL relationship in any but the most expensive of professional VTRs.

Servo systems

It has already been mentioned that it is essential to hold the tape speed and video head speed to very tight tolerances on both record and playback. A control track of pulses derived from the incoming video signal sync pulses is laid down on the tape during record and used to hold the video head drum in lock on playback (*Figure 4.24*). This type of servo system is called a drum servo and can be used to hold both head and tape speed constant. In more sophisticated VTRs a servo called a capstan servo is used to control the tape speed. The JVC HR3300 uses this dual servo system, whereas the Sony Betamax SL8000 relies on a head drum servo only.

In any servo system, if the feedback from the controlled object to the comparator is too high in relationship to the reference then the amplifier gain is reduced, and the system tends towards

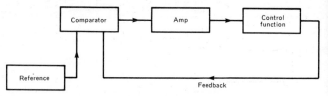

Figure 4.24. Basic servo system

he sound is played back through a hi-fi system rather than a
normal low-fi television set.

Tuners, timers and modulators

A main selling point of most domestic VTRs is their ability to be
able to record television programmes, especially in the absence
of the owner, and replay them on a normal television set so
tuners, timers and modulators are essential.

A television tuner built into a VTR such as the JVC HR3660 is
a conventional eight-channel-touch tuning circuit, covering (for
the UK market) the UHF channels 21 to 68. Thus to record a
television programme all you need is the aerial – not even a
television set! To watch the recording a black and white or
colour television is needed. Incidentally, as the television tuner
in the VTR is a colour one, the recording will always be in colour
so long as the programme is, regardless of the viewer's television
set. The VTR has an RF modulator built-in, which is in effect a
very small television transmitter. This takes the sound and vision
signals from the tape and modulates them onto an unused

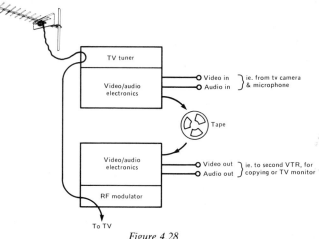

Figure 4.28

television channel. This output is fed into the television aerial socket.

Most VTRs also have separate video and audio outputs which can be fed to a TV monitor equipped with the correct socket (*Figure 4.28*). This method often gives a better quality picture as two stages of picture conversion are avoided. The video-in socket can be used with either a video camera or another VTR for tape copying. Some types of VTR do not have video in/out connectors and so any video signal fed to them must be fed in through the aerial socket as an RF signal. The Philips V100 and V200 cameras and N1700 VTR are examples of machines which rely on RF signals rather than baseband video signals, and the results produced by these combinations are, unfortunately, not of the best quality due to the extra signal processing involved.

Timers for making unattended recordings on VTRs have been getting more and more complex. The Philips N1500 of 1973 had a cooker-clock type timer, allowing a single recording to be made for up to 24 hours in advance of the setting time. The Sharp VC6300 of 1980 allows up to seven programmes on seven different television channels to be recorded at any period up to seven days in advance of the setting time. Most second generation VTRs have similar facilities. The use of solenoid operating controls simplifies the interfacing of timer to the recorder mechanism.

Contemporary tape format systems

This chapter will conclude by looking at the VHS and Beta formats in more detail, and also at the Philips V2000 format and some of the longitudinal video recorder systems which are under development.

The VHS system was developed by Matsushita of Japan as a true domestic VTR. The rival Betamax system from Sony is very similar but incompatible. It seems likely that both these formats will be with us for several years to come although the effects of the Philips V2000 machine on the market is difficult to estimate.

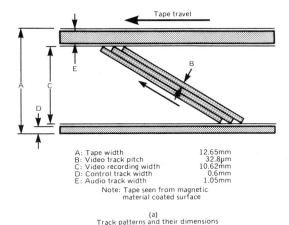

A: Tape width 12.65mm
B: Video track pitch 32.8μm
C: Video recording width 10.62mm
D: Control track width 0.6mm
E: Audio track width 1.05mm
Note: Tape seen from magnetic
material coated surface

(a)
Track patterns and their dimensions

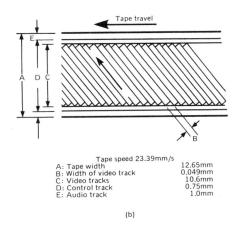

Tape speed 23.39mm/s
A: Tape width 12.65mm
B: Width of video track 0.049mm
C: Video tracks 10.6mm
D: Control track 0.75mm
E: Audio track 1.0mm

(b)

Figure 4.29. VTR track formats. (a) Beta. (b) VHS

Philips V2000

This is quite a revolutionary video system developed by Philips and Grundig and employing a flip-over cassette (VCC – Video Compact Cassette) rather like an overgrown audio cassette. Although half-inch tape is used, each video and audio track occupies only a quarter of an inch, which is the smallest tape width used in a mass-produced VTR to date. Playing times available run from 2×1 hours to 2×4 hours which promise the lowest running cost per hour of all the VTRs. Philips have already released the VR2020 and Grundig the 2×4 VTR, both based on the VCC – Video 2000 format. These VTRs are both second generation with fully-programmable timers, tuners and remote control, etc.

From the technical point of view the Video 2000 format is most interesting, as it has several novel features (*Figure 4.30*). The video head drum is 6.5 cm in diameter and is tilted to give a helical scanning tape path. There are two video heads tilted at $\pm 15°$ with respect to each other, giving a slant azimuth recording system, and no guard band. The video heads are 22 μm wide giving a total track width of 22.6 μm. Bear in mind that the average human hair is about 50 μm wide! The stereo audio tracks are 650 μm wide (325 μm left, 325 μm right), but are used as a single 650 μm wide mono sound track on the VR2020 VTR. In the centre of the tape there are two auxiliary tracks each 330 μm wide. These are not used in the VR2020, but could, Philips say, be used as cue-tracks for editing on future VTRs. There is, interestingly, no control track as found in every other type of domestic VTR. This is the track which has a squarewave pulse laid down on it during record, which is used to lock up the correct tape speed during playback. So how does the V2000 format manage? The answer is tied up with another feature missing from the VR2020, the tracking control. On other VTRs this is linked to circuitry which ensures that the video heads read the same tracks that they wrote. In the V2000 format synchronisation and tracking are performed by automatic circuitry which works in a very ingenious manner.

This system, which will also allow perfect slow, still and fast motion, while ensuring perfect machine compatibility, is what

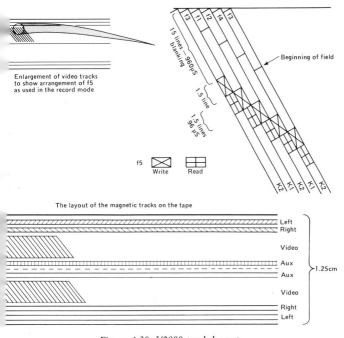

Enlargement of video tracks
to show arrangement of f5
as used in the record mode

15 lines — 960µS
blanking

1.5 line

1.5 lines
96 µS

f5   Write   Read

The layout of the magnetic tracks on the tape

Left
Right

Video

Aux

Aux   ⟩1.25cm

Video

Right
Left

Beginning of field

Figure 4.30. V2000 track layout

Philips call dynamic track following (DTF). The system first appeared in various broadcast VTRs but in conjunction with a conventional control track. It involves mounting the video heads on small pieces of piezo-electric crystal, which, when a voltage is applied, will bend either up or down as required. This enables the video heads to be shifted up or down to follow the video tracks (see *Figure 4.31*).

Briefly, DFT works like this. As in normal domestic VTRs, the incoming signal is filtered into its luma and chroma components, and the HF chroma converted to modulate a 625 kHz carrier. This is recorded along with the AM luma signal in a typical 'colour-under' system. However, DTF employs five further frequencies, which are recorded under the chroma carrier. These signals are put on during recording, and read in playback by the video heads. Signals derived from these frequencies are used to control the piezo-electric crystals. Control signals, written by the rotating video heads K1 and K2 are as follows:

$$K1 \quad F1 \quad 102 \text{ kHz}$$
$$K2 \quad F3 \quad 149 \text{ kHz}$$
$$K1 \quad F4 \quad 164 \text{ kHz}$$
$$K2 \quad F2 \quad 117 \text{ kHz}$$
$$\text{etc.}$$

During playback these tones are filtered out from the video signal. If the head is not exactly reading its 'own' video track then cross-talk signals from adjacent tracks will be present. If these cross-talk signals are mixed with the correct tone from the

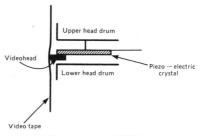

Figure 4.31. Section of V2000 head drum showing head and piezo-electric crystal

desired track then different signals are produced, which can be turned into control voltages to feed to the piezo-electric crystals. This will move the video heads to scan the correct track. An example will help to clarify the system.

If K1 is reading a track with F4 (164 kHz) but is slightly too low down, it scans part of the video track with an F2 tone (117 kHz) on it. The difference signal is 47 kHz. If the head is too high, then it picks up some of the F3 signal (149 kHz). This gives a difference signal of 15 kHz. For K2 the situation is reversed; if the head is too high the high frequency difference signal of 47 kHz is produced and if too low, 15 kHz is the result. If these signals are turned into control voltages the video heads can be perfectly aligned with the video tracks.

On recording, one video head is held in a nominally 'central' position and the second one is used in part of a control circuit. This is where the fifth tone frequency comes in. This tone, of 223 kHz, is written onto a 1.5 line period during the vertical blanking period as the signal is recorded. During the next 1.5 line period, (96µs), the video heads go into the 'read' mode, and measure the amplitude of the tone of the previous video track. This amplitude is turned into the control voltage which is fed to the other video head to correct for any scanning errors. That really sums up the essentials of the V2000 format, so now for a few details about the VR2000, the first VTR to use this format.

It is slightly smaller than the N1700, being about the same size as a VHS machine. All the tape transport controls are linked through a microprocessor to solenoids. The microprocessor also monitors and controls the speed of the video head drum. A calculator-style keyboard allows for easy programming of preset recording times and television channels. Up to 26 channels can be stored, which are selected by a self-seeking tuner. The VTR can be set to record up to five television programmes up to 16 days in advance. It will also change channels automatically if required. If a mains failure occurs the codes for the automatic recording sequence are stored in a type of programmable 'read-only memory' which will store the information for up to three months.

Besides Philips and Grundig, several other European companies have expressed an interest in marketing the V2000 format VTRs and Philips are offering free licences, as they did for their compact audio cassette, to encourage its adoption. A range of V2000 machines is promised by Philips for the future, including a portable, an editing VTR, a very basic and low-cost VTR and possibly a VTR equipped with an auto cassette changer, similar to that used by Sony with their Betamax VTRs.

Longitudinal video recording (LVR)

Longitudinal video recording VTRs are not, as might be supposed, a new idea as the earliest demonstrated colour VTR made by RCA in 1953 used fixed video heads and tape running at a very high speed. The main reason for the current interest in LVR systems is their lack of complex mechanical parts such as those found in the helical scan VTRs. This should not only increase the reliability but also reduce the cost. Leaving aside the earlier broadcast experiments using stationary video heads, BASF and Toshiba have shown an interest in using LVR as the basis for a domestic system.

BASF LVR system (LVR is a BASF registered trade name)

This system is only experimental at present and recent developments have cast doubt on its ever reaching the market place. A 600 m long, 8 mm wide and 8.5 μm thick video tape is housed in a plastic cassette and will give three hours of colour television recording on an LVR 180 tape. No take-up spool is used, as the tape comes with a leader length which is taken up by the VTR, rather in the manner of a self-threading cine projector. A very high tape-to-head speed is used and as the video head is fixed, this is obtained by running the tape at 4 m per second. This uses up one 600 m track in about 2.5 minutes! The three hour recording time is obtained by having the tape divided into 72 parallel tracks, each 100 μm wide. An automatic system ensures that the tape changes direction and the head scans the next track when the 'end' of a tape is reached. This process carries on until all 72 tracks are full. The change round time at the tape end is less than 100 ms, which, BASF claim, results in 'no perceptible interference to either sound or vision'.

Rapid access to any part of the tape is achieved by track jumping and a digital keypad is provided to enable the user to find the part of the programme required merely by keying-in the required tape-counter number.

The specification of the system is about average for domestic VTRs; with a 3 MHz bandwidth and a video signal-to-noise ratio of 42 dB. Stereo audio tracks will give a signal-to-noise pick-up of 56 dB, with a more or less flat frequency response from 40 Hz to 12.5 kHz. The high tape speed helps to account for this, having a wow and flutter figure of 0.01 DIN. Unlike other VTR manufac-turers BASF have concentrated their development plans around a portable VTR which can be linked to a mains power unit, battery recharger, TV tuner and programmable timer for use as a conventional time-shifting VTR.

Toshiba longitudinal video recorder

Toshiba have demonstrated their longitudinal video recorder system, confusingly called type V2020, in both American NTSC and UK PAL formats. Looking like a VHS or Betamax mains-operated VTR, this machine is capable of giving two hours' colour recording on a multi-track tape and is scheduled for UK sale in 1981. It employs 300 parallel tracks, each running for 24.6 seconds. It is expected that it will be on sale for around £300 (*Figure 4.32*).

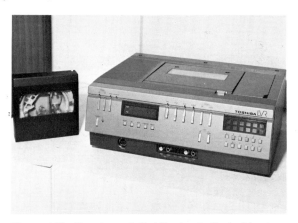

Figure 4.32. Experimental Toshiba longitudinal video tape recorder (Toshiba)

One important advantage of LVR systems is that tapes can be copied at high speed, like audio cassettes. Conventional helical-scan tapes are copied in real time; that is, a three-hour movie takes three hours to copy. Although experiments using high-speed copiers have been tried for various helical-scan formats, to date none has been entirely successful. For the pre-recorded software manufacturers a high-speed duplication system has a lot to commend it. However, the VHS and Betamax formats are very well established and LVR systems will have a job in replacing them in the television and audio shop windows.

Whatever happens in the way of new formats, the fact that almost 180 000 domestic VTRs were imported into the UK in 1979 seems to indicated that the British public have well and truly caught the video bug.

5 Video discs

The ability to record television pictures on discs has been a challenge to engineers from the earliest days of television. Baird demonstrated primitive video discs on his 30-line mechanical television system in 1928. Let us look at some of the supposed advantages of video discs and then at the technical aspects of some of the recent and current disc systems.

Initial interest in discs stems from Baird's need to have a way of preserving a copy of the output from his mechanical television camera. As the 30-line low-resolution television system used had a very low bandwidth, there was no problem involved in producing what were effectively audio-tone-encoded slow-scan television discs. These were conventional 78 rpm shellac discs and could be replayed on a normal gramophone, using a thorn needle. The audio output was then plugged into a Televisor in place of the normal radio loudspeaker signal. When the Baird television system died, the video disc story became dormant until the 1960s.

There were two stimuli pushing forward developments in the video disc field; first was the potential use of discs for action replays for the broadcasters and the second the sale of discs in the domestic markets. The first application, broadcast slow motion, etc, is now catered for by very expensive record/replay magnetic video disc systems, but the second, the domestic market, is still awaiting exploitation. One might well ask what is the point of domestic video discs. As a purely playback-only medium they are totally dependent on the supply of suitable software, that is, pre-recorded television programmes, available in quantity and at the right price. Most manufacturers envisage domestic video discs being used to play back big budget movies and DIY, cooking, keep fit and similar programmes. A salutary word of warning should be given at this point, as a playback-only video player, the EVR, tried for this market in the early 1970s and failed. It was too expensive and overestimated consumer interest. Let us hope that video discs fare better.

One can find references to over 40 different video disc systems, some of which have been on public sale, some which were pre-production prototypes, and some which were laboratory curiosities. Each falls into one of four categories based on the record/playback technology employed. These are: mechanical, as for the Baird and TeD systems; optical, the Philips VLP; capacitive, the Matsushita VISC and RCA's SelectaVision; and magnetic, MDR's experimental system. Some other experimental curiosities employing laser holography are around, but are not in any way commercial models. No-one has produced a commercial video disc system which can record as well as play back images. So the commerical success or otherwise of all current systems depends on a readily available supply of suitable software.

Mechanical systems

These have the advantage of being essentially low-technology, and therefore low-cost. The Baird system has already been mentioned. TelDec was the next mechanical system to be launched.

TelDec

1970 saw the demonstration of Teldec, a German/UK monochrome disc system, giving only five minutes of black and white television and associated sound on a floppy plastic disc. In this system from Telefunken/Decca, the picture information was recorded as an FM signal and encoded in a hill-and-dale manner (as opposed to the lateral and vertical manner of a conventional audio LP) in a microgroove spiral, there being 280 grooves per mm. This disc revolved at 1500 rpm or 25 revolutions per second

(PAL system). Corresponding times for the American, NTSC, system are 1800 rpm and 30 revolutions per second. The disc was brought into contact with the fixed-height pick-up head by floating on an air cushion derived from air forced under the disc.

In 1973, playing time was increased to ten minutes and a colour-compatible coding system was employed. The colour decoding system is interesting, as it employs a type of sequential colour circuitry, each colour having been recorded line by line *(Figure 5.1)*. Two 64 μs (one line) delay lines are needed to ensure that all these colour signals arrive at the matrix combiner at the same time. The production of master discs from which the consumer copies were pressed was usually done from a telecine transfer to a disc cutter running at 60 rpm instead of the 1500 rpm playback speed. This produced a very high quality master. Incidentally, although the copies were pressed from metal masters like audio LPs, they were stamped from a continuous strip of soft vinyl and not from blanks, like audio discs.

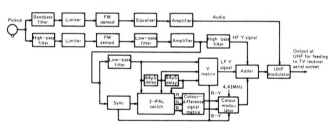

Figure 5.1. Block diagram of a TeD video disc player

The following year, 1974, the system was launched on the West German market with a cross-licensing agreement between Telefunken, and Sanyo and King Records of Japan. Unfortunately the system did not seem to catch on, possibly due to the rather limited choice of pre-recorded software and limited playing time. This latter problem was partly overcome by the use of a simple disc autochanger, giving over one hour's playing time. In 1975 the system was renamed TeD and stereo sound tracks were added. Now, however, apart from a limited use in medical education, TeD has apparently vanished from the scene.

Optical Systems

Video long play (VLP) or 'LaserVision'

The year which followed the launch of TelDec in 1970 saw the
demonstration of Philips video disc, a highly sophisticated
optical player system employing a laser (*Figure 5.2*). This system
is the most complex so far proposed for the domestic video disc
and in the USA it is sold as the Magnavox (Philips) and the
Pioneer 'Laserdisc' machines. In this system, the signals are

*Figure 5.2. Philips 'LaserVision' (VLP) video disc player
(Philips)*

encoded onto the disc so as to modulate a beam of light which
falls on the disc during playback. In practice, a series of pits of
variable length and repetition frequency are arranged in a spiral
which is scanned by a low power helium/neon laser, there being
no mechanical contact between the disc and the pick-up (*Figure
5.3*). This solves a whole range of problems, for example those
concerning scratches and dirt. The laser is arranged so as to be in
focus only on the pits, which are below the transparent surface of
the disc, so that a reasonable quantity of grease, fingerprints,
etc, on the disc do not affect the playback. An elaborate servo

Figure 5.3. A close look at the 'LaserVision' laser lens unit (Philips)

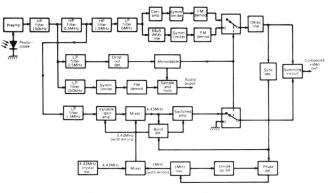

Figure 5.4. Block diagram of the circuits used in a 'LaserVision' (VLP) player

system ensures that the pick up follows the spiral of information, again relying on feed-back from the laser. Still-frame, fast and slow motion are all available, making the system ideal for commercial and educational use. As VLP has already been test-marketed in the USA – in 1978 in its NTSC form – let us look in some detail at the technical side of the system (*Figure 5.4*).

Technical aspects   A VLP disc is 300 mm in diameter – the same size as an ordinary audio LP – and comes in two forms; having either constant rotational velocity or constant linear velocity. In the first case the disc runs at 1800 rpm (NTSC)/1500 rpm (PAL) and has two fields (one frame) per revolution. This means that the disc rotational speed is equal to the frame frequency, making still picture and fast/slow motion easily obtainable. As the field pulses of the television signals occur in the same part of the disc, regardless of which groove the pick-up is tracking, fast motion can be obtained by missing out each alternate field. Still pictures are obtained by repeating the same field, and so on (see *Figure 5.5*). The pick-up uses the field blanking period to change grooves so that no picture disturbance is seen. In this mode the disc has a playing time of 30 minutes per side, with each track having a pitch of 2μm. The pressed disc is coated with a thin layer of reflective metal to improve its reflective qualities and this is protected by a layer of perspex-like transparent material.

The original goal of Philip's team was to produce a disc with 60 minutes playing time per disc, but it was soon realised that this would not be enough for the movies, etc., so a means of increasing the playing time was sought. The answer was to run the disc at a slower, but varying speed, around 600 rpm (NTSC) or 500 rpm (PAL). In this mode the linear velocity of the disc relative to the pick-up arm is kept constant giving 55 minutes per side playing time in exchange for loss of still-frame, fast and slow motion, etc. This is because the television frames occupy the same track length regardless of how far they are from the disc's centre and are packed in at the highest possible density, giving between two and six frames per revolution. The loss of stills does not seem to be very important for watching movies, so that by having the two systems incorporated in single player, Philips appear to have solved the problem of which market, educational/

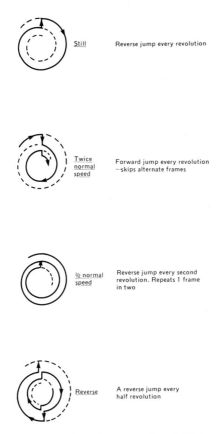

Still — Reverse jump every revolution

Twice normal speed — Forward jump every revolution – skips alternate frames

½ normal speed — Reverse jump every second revolution. Repeats 1 frame in two

Reverse — A reverse jump every half revolution

Figure 5.5. The Philips 'LaserVision' CAV 'active play' disc allows for all these possibilities by allowing two jumps per revolution in the field blanking periods

commercial or domestic, to go for; their answer is both! Current versions of the player incorporate auto-switching which detects the type of disc loaded and alters the speed accordingly.

The ability to display still frames can be put to good use in the educational market where around 45000 separate colour stills could be stored on each side of the disc. As each frame is uniquely numbered, a go-to remote control will allow rapid (about three seconds) access to any one frame. Such a still store could hold text-type records, photographs, diagrams, etc.

VLP disc mastering   VLP discs are produced by a variation the conventional audio disc-pressing technique of using a metal stamp to impress information onto plastic blanks. The master disc is cut onto a glass disc by a special high-powered laser. Interestingly, the master disc is spun at 25 rps (PAL) during cutting, exactly the same as the playback speed. This encoded glass disc is then used to produce a pressing mould by an electroplating technique, just as for audio LPs.

It will be noted that with a rotation speed of 25 rps and the encoding system employed by Philips, the normal video spectrum of 25 Hz to 5.5 MHz cannot be successfully recorded throughout the disc. The problem is most marked towards the centre of the disc, due to the shortness of each rotation and hence the high packing density of the signal information. Towards the outer edge of the disc, full bandwidth recording would be possible. In practice, Philips have adopted a cut-off frequency of around 3 MHz. The colour subcarrier is removed from 4.43 MHz to 1 MHz (PAL), while limiting the total bandwidth of the colour signal to ± 0.5 MHz. This colour-under coding system is similar to that employed in slow-speed domestic video tape recorders. The stereo sound signal is also recorded as two-frequency (around 250 kHz) FM signals. Sophisticated signal processing is employed to make sure that cross-talk interference is avoided. These stereo sound signals are available from the player for feeding through a separate hi-fi system to get better quality sound than that possible from the normal television set. Certainly the picture quality of a demonstration PAL version of the system (1980) was very high, although there are considerable problems involved in pressing a satisfactory percentage of discs. Philips are using the Mullard Valve factory in Blackburn, UK, for their PAL disc-production plant.

Other optical systems

Besides Philips and its American companion company, Magnavox, various other companies have demonstrated an interest in optical disc systems. Pioneer, Sony, Sanyo, Trio, Grundig, IBM and Thompson/CSF have all adopted the Philips VLP format, while Matsushita and Bosch have demonstrated their own (incompatible) disc players. Philips, Polygram, Pioneer Artists and InterVision (UK) have also signed up to supply software for the VLP format. The main disadvantage with all these optical systems is that they rely on very high technology and are therefore comparatively expensive.

Capacitive systems

Both RCA in the USA and JVC in Japan have adopted capacitive systems for their video disc players, which unfortunately are incompatible. In these, sound and vision signals are encoded as changes in local capacitance in the disc surface, which are then detected upon playback by a capacitive pick-up. In effect the disc acts as one plate and the pick-up as the other plate of a capacitor.

RCA SelectaVision

The RCA SelectaVision, or CED (capacitive electronic disc) as it now seems to be called, is a relatively low-cost player which has been in development since the 1950s (*Figure 5.6*). By 1978 the stage was reached when the disc format had been finalised and the several hundred thousand test discs had been pressed. The SFT100 player was launched in the USA in 1981, with a European launch promised for 1982, at a price of around £250. A 300 mm disc, spinning at 450 rpm NTSC (500 rpm PAL) is used, giving 60 minutes' playing time per side. Colour video and associated audio signals are encoded in the form of capacitive variations as transverse slots of varying width and periodicity impressed in the bottom of the record's spiral groove. The tip of the metal/diamond stylus serves as a capacitive probe to recover the signal (*Figure 5.7*). This stylus tracks across the disc in the spiral groove in the same way as a conventional audio LP. As the stylus is in physical contact with the disc a thin layer of lubricant is added to it to reduce wear and tear. The disc is packed in a caddy to provide further protection – a disc being removed automatically once the caddy has been inserted into the player. As six fields (eight NTSC) of picture information are stored on each revolution, still, fast and slow motion are not possible, unlike Philips VLP, so the SelectaVision system is not suitable for information retrieval.

Mastering RCA discs   RCA master video discs are produced, not by laser, but by an electro-mechanical disc cutter. This device is fed with suitably encoded audio, luma and chroma signals and cuts a vee-shaped groove into the copper blank; simultaneously it cuts the signal elements in the bottom of the groove. The master recording is made in real-time; that is, at the rotational speed of 450 rpm (NTSC). This copper master is then used to produce moulds by an electro-plating technique, and these are used to press out the consumer discs. These discs are made of familiar LP-type PVC, but impregnated with conductive carbon granules. RCA have also developed optical (laser) and electron beam recording techniques which have been demonstrated on a laboratory scale. As with Philips VLP a colour-under encoding system employed with a colour frequency of 1.53 MHz (NTSC) being used (*Figure 5.8*).

The marketing plans are well advanced for the CED player to be introduced into the UK. GEC are a licensee for player manufacturing in the UK, with RCA Records and ACC (previously ATV) supplying software. In the States, CBS will provide programme material and Zenith, Sharp, Hitachi and Sanyo have demonstrated an interest in providing the players to this format.

Figure 5.6. RCA CED video disc player (RCA)

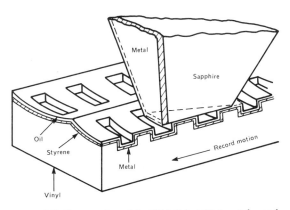

Figure 5.7. Construction of the RCA SelectaVision stylus and disc surface. This is a development version only. The current production version employs a diamond/metal stylus and a conductive PVC disc with no styrene or metal, only a thin oil coating

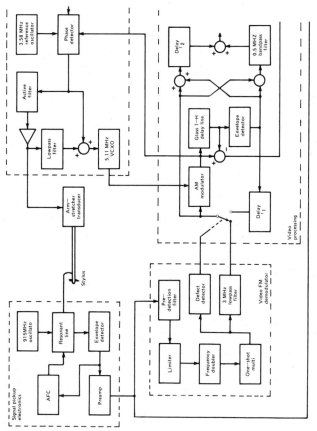

Figure 5.8. RCA CED player block diagram, NTSC version

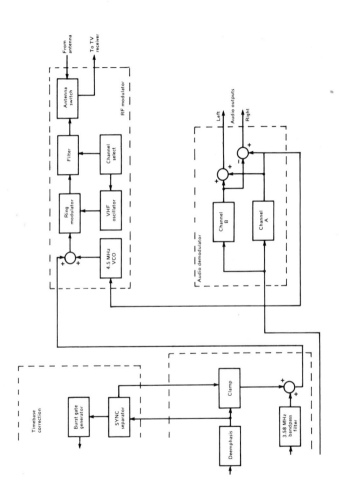

JVC VHD

JVC's video home disc (VHD) player is a relative newcomer to the market, having announced in 1978 and only demonstrated in the UK (in NTSC form) in 1980 (see *Figure 5.9*). Like RCA's SelectaVision, it relies on capacitive technology, thus promising a lower cost than VLP. Unlike SelectaVision, JVC originally specified that the player should reproduce both video discs and digital audio discs, when they were developed. (Philips envisage two separate players, one for video and one for audio discs.)

Figure 5.9. JVC VHD video disc player (JVC)

JVC also intend the player to be aimed at both the industrial (still frames, texts, etc). and the home (long-playing movies' market). It was also envisaged that highly reliable, relatively unsophisticated electronics and mechanics should be employed. 300 mm diameter, double-sided, conductive PVC discs are used, rotating at 900 rpm (NTSC; no PAL version as yet), giving 60 minutes' playing time per side. The picture and sound information are recorded in the form of pits in the surface of the plastic disc, arranged in a spiral. Unlike an audio LP, there is however no groove, the surface of the disc being smooth. The sapphire stylus is made to follow the spiral by a servo-tracking system, which gets its information from additional pits adjacent to the main information signal (*Figure 5.10*). The servo system which controls the pick-up arm has not only to be very fast in responding to control signals, but also able to move the pick-up in both the vertical and horizontal planes. A sapphire stylus is

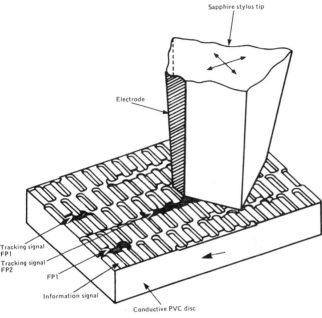

Figure 5.10. VHD stylus

mounted at the end of a cantilevered arm, which has a small permanent magnet at the other end. A coil of an electromagnet is closely wound around the fixed magnet and next to this are a pair of anti-phase vertical coils (*Figure 5.11*). As the currents flowing through these coils are derived from the time-base error and tracking signal respectively, the position of the arm may be controlled quite easily. Tracking coils are also used to move the stylus to any selected part of the disc for rapid access to information. A sliding stylus has about ten times the contact area of a conventional groove-following stylus, thus helping to pro-long the life of both stylus and disc. As in the Selectavision system, the disc is housed in a caddy, which is posted into the player and automatically unloaded.

Mastering VHD discs   The master discs for VHD are cut using a laser, as shown in *Figure 5.12*. A flat glass disc coated with photographic emulsion is spun at 900 rpm and illuminated with a laser which tracks across the surface. An arrangement of mirrors and optical splitters is used to provide a composite beam which carries sound, vision and tracking signals. A lens is used to converge these beams onto the disc surface. A glass disc is developed and a metal master produced. The process is repeated for the second side and the metal master is used for pressing copies of discs.

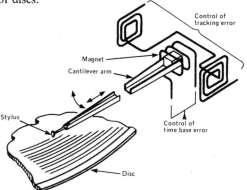

Figure 5.11. VHD stylus tracking system

Although only demonstrated in NTSC form to date, JVC are claiming that it will be ready for marketing in the winter of 1981, by which time a list of 200 programmes should already be available. This rapid introduction is surprising as JVC claim the player will give still, fast and slow-motion pictures – which is difficult to achieve as four fields of picture are recorded in each revolution. Using current technology, this would require an expensive video frame store occupying several racks of equipment. Possibly JVC hope to miniaturise this type of equipment and incorporate it as an add-on to the player. Certainly the UK

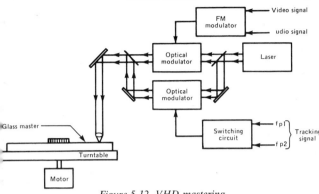

Figure 5.12. VHD mastering

demonstration in 1980 relied on a commercial frame store to achieve the still effects.

Matsushita, Panasonic and Quasar – all related companies to JVC – are backing VHD, while in the UK Thorn–EMI have entered into an agreement with JVC over VHD. In the USA, GEC have done likewise. Toshiba will almost certainly follow suit, being another JVC-related company.

Magnetic recording

With current technology, this is the only practical method of providing both recording and playback from a single unit; all other techniques are suitable for replay use only. Magnetic disc records have been used in professional television for many years and have been used to provide sports' stills, action replays, etc. The Ampex HS 2000 was one of the first commercial broadcast disc recorder/players and continuously records, reads and re-records a 45 second chunk of television programme onto a magnetic disc. Obviously this type of equipment is not suitable for the domestic market. Up to the time of writing the German/French MDR (magnetic disc recorder) is the only domestic type of machine to have been demonstrated – in 1974. Employing a double-sided 305 mm diameter disc, running at 156 rpm, it gave around 20 minutes' playing time per side. Price levels in 1976 for player/recorders were expected to be about £375, with discs at

£5. The system was never marketed and now seems to have vanished.

The future

Back in 1974 Philips were 'hoping to market (VLP) this year' and mass-produce 'within a few years'. They are now (in 1980) saying the VLP will be on sale in the UK in 1981. It is clear however that, even allowing for experimental record/playback disc systems, most manufacturer's efforts are being directed into player-only devices and relying on domestic video tape recorders to provide the recording facilities people require. It is also clear that any disc system will only survive if an adequate range of software is available at realistic prices (say £5 – £10). If this condition is met, then whichever company gets a video disc player onto the UK market first is likely to make a killing.

To conclude this chapter, Tables 5.1, 5.2 and 5.3 list respectively the chronology of video disc development, the principal characteristics of several systems and a detailed technical comparison of the specifications of three video disc systems.

Table 5.1. The chronology of the development of video disc systems

1927	Baird Radiovision demonstrated
1935	Baird Radiovision discs on sale
1971	Teldec demonstrated, 5 mins monochrome
1972	EVR abandoned and Philips VCR launched
1972	Philips VLP announced
1973	TelDec demonstrated, 10 mins colour
1974	TelDec launched on German market, with cross-licensing agreement with Sanyo and King Records of Japan
1974	Philips VLP 'hope to market this year, (1974)' and 'mass-produce within a few years'
1975	MCA laser 'Discovision', 'to be launched in 1975', abandoned and merged with Philips VLP
1975	Teldec renamed TeD, and has stereo sound
1977	RCA 'SelectaVision' presses 200,000 test discs
1978	RCA 'SelectaVision' launch imminent
1978	VLP/Discovision on sale in Atlanta, USA
1979	Cross-patent agreement between Philips and other European, US and Japanese manufacturers concerning video discs
1980	Philips UK Blackburn plant scheduled to go on-stream pressing VLP discs
1981	RCA 'SelectaVision' launched in the USA

Table 5.2. The principal characteristics of several video disc systems

Manufacturers	Disc name	System	Playing time	Rotational speed rpm	Colour standard	Disc material
Baird TV Development Co	Radiovision	Mechanical	7 mins	78	–	Shellac disc
AEG-Telefunken Decca	TelDec (TeD)	Mechanical	20 mins	450	PAL	Floppy plastic disc
Philips/MCA	VLP/ Discovision	Laser optical	2 hrs	1800/600 1500/500	NTSC PAL	Metallised reflective plastic
RCA	SelectaVision	Capacitance Mechanical	2 hrs	450 500	NTSC PAL	Conductive PVC
JVC	Video Home Disc	Capacitance	2 hrs	900	NTSC	?
Matsushita	VISC	Mechanical	2 hrs	450	NTSC	?

Table 5.3. Comparison of video disc specifications

Specified system	Philips VLP PAL	RCA SelectaVision PAL	JVC VHD NTSC
Disc diameter	305mm	305mm	26cm
Disc thickness	2.2mm	2mm (centre and rim)	
Centre hole diameter	37mm	37mm	
Recorded band	130mm to 290mm	144.3 to 76.2mm radius (68.6mm)	
Rotation rate	(1,500 to 500) rev/minute	500 rev/minute	900 rev/minute
Fields per rev	2 (2 to 6)	6	4
Sides	Two	Two	Two
Duration per side	30 minutes (60)	60 minutes	60 minutes
Cutting transducer	Laser HeNe 100mW	Electromechanical	Laser
Reading transducer	Laser HeNe 1mW	Capacitive	Capacitive
Playback tracking	Optical servo	Mechanical groove	Electronic servo
Recorded signal	6.5–7.9MHz	4.3–6.3MHz FM	4.8–6.6MHz FM
Luma bandwidth	4.3MHz	3MHz	3.1MHz
Chroma bandwidth	0.5MHz	0.5MHz	
Video noise	−48dB	−48dB (CCIR weighted)	−42dB
Audio channels	Two	Two	Two
Audio carrier	0.68 and 1.06MHz	711 or 898kHz	
Audio carrier deviation	±100kHz	±50kHz	
Audio bandwidth	40kHz to 20kHz	20kHz	20kHz
Audio THD	0.3%		
Audio channel separation	60dB		
Audio noise	−55dB	−55dB approx.	−60dB
Disc material	Plastic/metal	Oiled conductive PVC	Conductive PVC
Track pitch	1.6μm	2.67μm	1.35μm
Key year	1972	1975	1978

6 Videotext

Videotext is the generic name given to all the systems which are designed to display 'pages' of text and graphics on television sets. The term 'page' usually means a 'screenfull' of still text instead of moving pictures. There are a number of different videotext systems available throughout the world, of which the British 'Teletext' system was the first. As Teletext was the original videotext system and as it is probably the most familiar to the general public, we will start our examination there.

Teletext

This is the specific name given to the videotext services generated by the BBC and ITV companies. That transmitted by the BBC is called 'Ceefax' (see *Facts*) and that by ITV 'Oracle'. These services provide news and information which can be received and displayed by specially designed or modified television sets as pages of text on the screen. The information is transmitted by the broadcasters along with the normal television programmes and the Teletext set or decoder extracts data and transforms them into lines of text or simple graphics. Before discussing how Teletext is transmitted and decoded, let us first look briefly at some of the types of information available to Teletext decoder-equipped viewers.

The full index listing all the pages of information on BBC 1 alone would take up a complete page of this book but *Figure 6.1* gives some of the major subject headings. The information includes the news, weather, sport, current affairs, and similar sorts of 'newspaper' type information. The BBC 2 Teletext 'magazine', as a set of pages is called, tends to include more background information to current events as well as book and film reviews, recipes, reports on new cars, educational quizzes, etc. The ITV magazines are similar, but contain even more pages. So, if you are equipped with a Teletext set, you can examine all sorts of information at the touch of a button! How is this done?

Figure 6.1. (a) The general index page of ITV's Oracle videotext system (Closed Circuit Consultants)

Figure 6.1. (b) The index page of Ceefax, the BBC's videotext system (Closed Circuit Consultants)

How Teletext works

Teletext, in the form of BBC's Ceefax and ITV's Oracle has a joint specification, even though both systems were originally developed separately. This compatible specification was agreed by both broadcasting authorities in January 1974, and experimental transmissions to a very limited number of viewers commenced. The specification was amended in 1976 to allow for the addition of some new features, and the world's first public videotext service was inaugurated. Teletext is transmitted along with the normal TV programmes and decoded by special TV sets and displayed as pages of text. This extra information is carried in the television signal in a very ingenious way, using some of the spare lines of the television picture.

A conventional television picture is displayed upon the CRT by means of a method called raster scan. This entails building up the picture by scanning the screen line by line with an electron beam. This scanning is controlled by the line timebase, producing a linear left to right sweep, and the field timebase, producing a linear top to bottom sweep. Each line takes 64 µs to scan, and a field, of 312½ lines, 20 ms. A second field is interlaced with the first, but shifted by half a line, to provide the familiar 625-line colour picture. The interlacing is done to reduce the picture flicker without increasing the bandwidth of the transmitted signal. Although 625 lines are available in the signal, not all are used to carry picture information, as 25 per field are needed to allow for the blanking period, that is, when the electron beam moves from bottom-right to top-left of the CRT. This means that there are some 50 spare lines in the television picture, which can be used to carry various extra signals. In fact some of these lines are already used for carrying signals such as ITS (insertion test signals), for checking television system performance and SLICE (Source Label Indication and Control Equipment), for showing the broadcasters the originating studio of the television programmes. Initially, therefore, four lines, numbers 17 and 18 in the even field and 330 and 331 in the odd field, have been allocated for Teletext services, although this number could be increased if need be. If more lines were used more information could be transmitted, or the access time to locate a specific page could be reduced – more about this later. *Figure 6.2* shows the television lines in the field blanking period and how the Teletext signal is

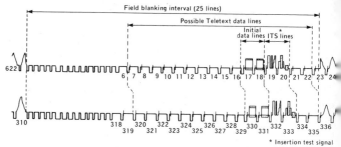

Figure 6.2 Field blanking waveforms showing Teletext data lines

carried. This signal consists of digital, that is, binary, information which can be extracted from the composite television waveform by the decoder, decoded into text information and displayed.

The following sections will show how text can be encoded, transmitted and decoded.

Digital transmission

Normal television signals are said to be analogue in nature; that is, the voltage amplitude of the signal may be at any level between maximum or minimum of that system at any one time, and in a television system that value will represent a grey value between black and peak white. A digital signal, as in *Figure 6.3.(a)* will always be at either zero or one; there is no intermediate level. Some systems of encoding and decoding is needed to put analogue information into, and extract it from, a digital system. Digital systems are ideal, however, for transmitting coded information, which is exactly what happens in Teletext systems.

Digital codes for alphanumeric characters are transmitted, decoded in the receiver and used to generate characters from a

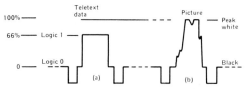

Figure 6.3. Video signals. (a) Teletext. (b) Picture

character generator in the Teletext decoder in the television set. The structure of the Teletext message is relatively simple. Each data line, (17 and 18, and 330 and 331) carries a series of 360 digital pulses, arranged in a specific order. In practice this consists of 16 digits of synchronising clock information, followed by eight digits of frame synchronising information. The magazine and row address follow, occupying 16 digits. This is normally followed by 320 digits which represent 40 characters. These 40 characters represent a complete row of Teletext information on the display screen.

For those interested in the very technical side of things, Teletext signals are said to be eight-bit in nature. This means that eight binary digits (bits) make up a complete 'word' or byte; in this case a character. A total of 45 bytes is needed for a complete row of text, and as a row of text occupies a single line scan (17, 18, 330 or 331) then the data transmission rate is 6.9375 megabits per second, with a time period of 144 ns per bit. *Figure 6.4* gives the layout of Teletext data on a television line, and details the sequencing of the information.

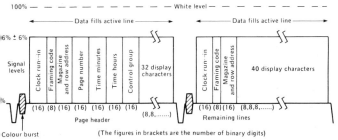

Figure 6.4. Layout of Teletext data on a television line

Data organisation

Figure 6.5 is a photograph of a typical page of Teletext information, and can be seen to consist of a page header, displaying page number, selected magazine name, page being received, day, date, month, television channel and real-time in hours, minutes and seconds. The clock signal, incidentally, is derived from a caesium standard, and is therefore very accurate indeed.

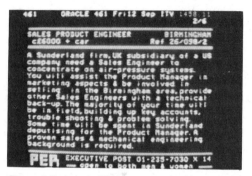

Figure 6.5. A typical Teletext page, in this case a job vacancy (Closed Circuit Consultants)

It is important to realise that although all the pages in a Teletext magazine are broadcast continuously, at about half-second intervals, the decoder in the viewer's set 'grabs' the specified page the viewer has keyed in from his keyboard. The time taken to display the specified page may thus take up to about 23 seconds, depending where in the sequence of pages the viewer keys-in his request. From this it can be seen that it is most important that the page header is received and decoded correctly by the receiver, or else the entire page of information may be lost. If an error occurs elsewhere in the page, than either a row or character may be lost or garbled, but the sense of the whole message will probably not be lost. Certain methods are used to ensure that errors in transmission and decoding do not interfere with the display of information too drastically.

Error protection

It has already been shown that Teletext information is arranged in eight-bit bytes or words. Seven of these eight bits carry characters and similar information, but the eighth is a special error-detecting bit called a parity bit. The state (either logic '1' or '0') is chosen for each word, so the total number of '1' bits is always odd. This is called 'odd parity.' For example, if a word consisted of five '0's and two '1's, then the parity bit would be a '1', making three '1's in total. A circuit in the decoder counts the parity bits, and if they are even an error in the preceding word is suspected, and it is rejected. As a result a blank space will appear on the screen. Such errors can be caused by interference bits getting into the Teletext system. The parity bit is also used to resynchronise the decoder clock to the data clock during each byte, but how this is done is beyond the scope of this book. It can be seen that parity error-checking cannot correct errors nor detect multiple errors which cancel each other out, for example a transposition of digits. For this reason, a better, but more space-consuming system of error protection is employed to protect the vital page header and row address.

'Hamming codes,' named after R. W. Hamming of Bell Telephones of the USA, can not only detect errors, but also provide some degree of error correction as well. In a Hamming-protected address code, for example, only four of the eight bits in the byte would carry data, the remaining four being parity codes. *Figure 6.6* shows the arrangement of normal and Hamming-protected Teletext bytes; *Figure 6.7* shows how these are used to check and correct errors. It can be seen that although bit 8 is used as a normal parity check, it is also used, with the other

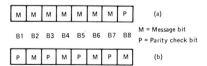

Figure 6.6. Teletext data bytes. (a) Normal text data. (b) Hamming-code address data

three parity bits, to carry out multiple checks on the four data bits. Thus a single-bit error can be detected and corrected. Multiple errors result in the entire byte being rejected. This results in rows of pages being deleted, which is better than incorrect information being displayed.

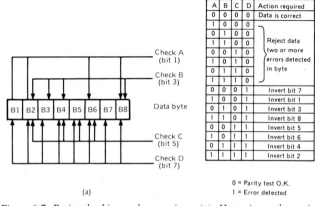

A	B	C	D	Action required
0	0	0	0	Data is correct
1	0	0	0	Reject data two or more errors detected in byte
0	1	0	0	
1	1	0	0	
0	0	1	0	
1	0	1	0	
0	1	1	0	
1	1	1	0	
0	0	0	1	Invert bit 7
1	0	0	1	Invert bit 1
0	1	0	1	Invert bit 3
1	1	0	1	Invert bit 8
0	0	1	1	Invert bit 5
1	0	1	1	Invert bit 6
0	1	1	1	Invert bit 4
1	1	1	1	Invert bit 2

0 = Parity test O.K.
1 = Error detected

(a)

Figure 6.7. Parity checking and correction. (a) Hamming-code parity checks. (b) Results of parity tests and corrective action required

Having looked at how the data are transmitted and how it is arranged and protected against errors, let us see how a viewer could select a specific page and how it would be decoded and displayed.

Page selection

As was previously mentioned, all pages of a magazine are transmitted sequentially, at about half-second intervals, taking around 20 – 30 seconds to transmit a complete magazine. The viewer can key in the number of any desired page and when Teletext data with that page number are received, they are identified and stored line by line, until a complete page is formed, when it will be displayed.

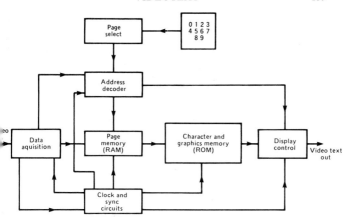

Figure 6.8. Teletext decoder block diagram

The first problem of a decoder is to identify and remove Teletext data from the normal picture information. *Figure 6.8* shows the layout of a typical Teletext decoder and shows how the data acquisition section is related to the data selection, page memory and display sections. The video signal is passed through a data slicer, which converts any signal above about 50 per cent of the peak-to-peak maximum to a logic '1' and anything below to logic '0'; often + volts and − volts respectively. Early decoders used integrated circuit comparators but current models often employ adaptive data slicers which automatically cope with changes in the d.c. level of the video signal caused by changes in temperature and/or signal strength.

As the video information on all lines processed is in this manner, some method of identifying Teletext lines is required to separate them from rubbish produced by slicing television signal lines. A simple monostable circuit can be used to open a 'window' during which data are accepted and it can be timed from the field synchronising pulse. The decoder should now have produced a string of data pulses which now need to be identified as individual bits. In order for this to be done, the logic level of the data stream must be sampled during each bit period. An on-board clock in the decoder can do this, but to ensure that it takes samples at the right time, it needs not only to produce pulses at 6.9375 MHz (the data bit rate) but also to be synchronised to the incoming data. The first two bytes in each line of Teletext data are clock words which lock the internal clock to the data rate clock. Having synchronised the on-board clock to the data, the next thing to be done is to locate the start of the first data word by using eight bit framing code. This is used as a timing reference from which the position of every other data bit in the row can be determined. Finally, the data is converted from serial to eight-bit parallel form to allow it to be decoded and stored more easily. This can be envisaged as a way of slowing down the data stream rate.

Having arranged the data into sequence, it is now possible to select out the data required for any specific page from the data stream. It will be recalled that each page of information is uniquely identified by a binary code, as are the rows in the text. It might be thought that the page address would come first in the data stream, but in fact it is the row address which comes after the framing code. A page of text consists of 24 rows of text, each consisting of up to 40 characters. The two bytes (16 bits) which follow the framing code label the lines from 0 to 23, so that the decoder can arrange them in order on the screen. The page address is transmitted only on the first line of a new page, and reduces the number of characters which can be carried on this

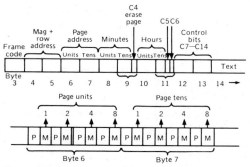

Figure 6.9. Arrangement of data bits for a page header

line. *Figure 6.9* shows the arrangement of the data bits for a page header. A decoder compares the desired page number as keyed-in by the user with the received page number, and when the two are coincident, starts to store rows of text into page memory. When a second page header is received, the decoder assumes that the stored page is complete and displays it.

Saving space and time

A way of reducing the access time (the time the viewer needs to wait for the desired page to be displayed) is to ensure that any rows of text which are blank do not have to be transmitted in full, that is as a row of blank spaces. The design of the decoder is therefore arranged so as to insert rows of blank text where no characters are transmitted. This process can result in a time saving of around 20 – 25 per cent but brings with it some further problems. If a new page, has only say lines 7, 11 and 20 containing any text then the other lines on the previous page will be left, resulting in a garbled page. To prevent this, an erase-control bit is included and transmitted with the time code address in the page header. This erases the old page from memory before a new one is written in.

Character display

It will be recalled that the picture on the television screen is formed by the electron beam scanning lines of phosphor dots. The specification for Teletext calls for characters to be formed

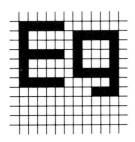

Figure 6.10. 10×6 dot matrix

from a box of 10×6 dots as shown in *Figure 6.10*. In practice most characters fit into a 5×7 box, but Y and G, for example, have descenders which need space below the main line for symbols. One vertical and one horizontal space is left around each character to separate it from the next.

Character rounding

A way of improving the legibility of the 5×9 characters has been devised which relies on the two interlaced scans of the television

				B7	0	0	0	0	1	1	1	1
				B6	0	0	1	1	0	0	1	1
				B5	0	1	0	1	0	1	0	1
B4	B3	B2	B1									
0	0	0	0				Sp	0	@	P	—	p
0	0	0	1				!	1	A	Q	a	q
0	0	1	0				"	2	B	R	b	r
0	0	1	1				£	3	C	S	c	s
0	1	0	0				$	4	D	T	d	t
0	1	0	1		Codes in these		%	5	E	U	e	u
0	1	1	0		two columns		&	6	F	V	f	v
0	1	1	1		are for control		'	7	G	W	g	w
1	0	0	0		and are		(	8	H	X	h	x
1	0	0	1		not displayed		)	9	I	Y	i	y
1	0	1	0				*	:	J	Z	j	z
1	0	1	1				+	;	K	←	k	¼
1	1	0	0				,	<	L	½	l	‖
1	1	0	1				—	=	M	→	m	¾
1	1	1	0				.	>	N	↑	n	÷
1	1	1	1				/	?	O	#	o	■

Figure 6.11. Table of Teletext symbols and their associated codes

raster. This method is particularly effective wtih diagonal letters such as V or A. Under normal circumstances the dot patterns on alternate scans would be identical, but in the character rounding mode a half-length dot is added on the other field, either before or after the full-sized dot.

Character generating

One of the innovations which has made Teletext possible is that the system can transmit codes for characters rather than actual characters. This reduces the amount of information and hence the signal bandwidth considerably. The codes are used to access pre-programmed characters from a ROM (read-only memory). *Figure 6.11* shows the codes and characters associated with the Teletext specification.

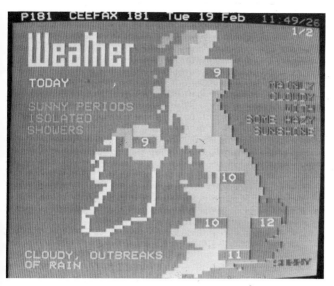

Figure 6.12. The weather map showing the use of contiguous graphics (BBC)

Graphics

Relatively simple graphic displays can be produced by Teletext to supplement the alphanumeric information. A typical example of this feature would be a UK weather map. (*Figures 6.12 and 6.13*). The graphics display is built up in a similar manner to that for characters, but using a coarser (lower resolution) matrix.

Figure 6.13. A similar map but displyed on an early decoder not equipped to display contiguous graphics. Note the 'gaps' in it (Closed Circuit Consultants)

Figure 6.14 shows the 3 × 2 shape used; this effectively produces an 80 line × 72 row picture across the television screen. Bit 7 is used for the lower right-hand side, not bit 6, as this is a control bit employed to tell the receiver to switch between graphics and alphanumeric characters. Consequently, if the graphics' control character appears in the row header, graphic output will be produced for that row. If it does not appear, alphanumerics are produced. *Figure 6.15* shows the complete font set from the graphics' generator and the associated control codes.

B1	B2
B3	B4
B5	B7

Figure 6.14. The graphics matrix and allocation of bits to the segments

Colour

As well as generating white characters on a black background, Teletext can also produce six-colour displays. *Figure 6.15* also shows the codes for colour alphanumerics and backgrounds. Although colour is not essential to Teletext, it does produce a more interesting display and can be useful in differentiating blocks of text, titles, maps, etc. As with graphics, special control codes are employed, which tell the decoder to produce characters or graphics of the specified colour. In the early decoders

				B7	0	0	0	0	1	1	1	1
			B6	0	0	1	1	0	0	1	1
			B5	0	1	0	1	0	1	0	1
B4	B3	B2	B1	0	1	2	3	4	5	6	7
0	0	0	0	NUL	DLE	▦	▦	@	P	▦	▦
0	0	0	1	ALPHA RED	GRAPHICS RED	▦	▦	A	Q	▦	▦
0	0	1	0	ALPHA GREEN	GRAPHICS GREEN	▦	▦	B	R	▦	▦
0	0	1	1	ALPHA YELLOW	GRAPHICS YELLOW	▦	▦	C	S	▦	▦
0	1	0	0	ALPHA BLUE	GRAPHICS BLUE	▦	▦	D	T	▦	▦
0	1	0	1	ALPHA MAGENTA	GRAPHICS MAGENTA	▦	▦	E	U	▦	▦
0	1	1	0	ALPHA CYAN	GRAPHICS CYAN	▦	▦	F	V	▦	▦
0	1	1	1	ALPHA WHITE	GRAPHICS WHITE	▦	▦	G	W	▦	▦
1	0	0	0	FLASH	CONCEAL	▦	▦	H	X	▦	▦
1	0	0	1	STEADY	CONTIGUOUS GRAPHICS	▦	▦	I	Y	▦	▦
1	0	1	0	END BOX	SEPARATED GRAPHICS	▦	▦	J	Z	▦	▦
1	0	1	1	START BOX	ESC	▦	▦	K	←	▦	▦
1	1	0	0	NORMAL HEIGHT	BLACK BACKGROUND	▦	▦	L	½	▦	▦
1	1	0	1	DOUBLE HEIGHT	NEW BACKGROUND	▦	▦	M	→	▦	▦
1	1	1	0	SO	HOLD GRAPHICS	▦	▦	N	↑	▦	▦
1	1	1	1	SI	RELEASE GRAPHICS	▦	▦	O	#	▦	▦

Figure 6.15. Symbol and code table for graphics and control

used during the trial period of the operation, the system use⬦
meant that if a change of colour occurred along any line, a black
gap was left between the colour changes. This reduces the
effectiveness of the graphics and the current Teletext specification employs a 'graphics-hold' which ensures that the previous
graphic symbol is repeated when the change-colour code is
detected and this gives a smooth transition from one colour to
the next. Colour can also be used as an alternative to the black
background upon which the characters are displayed; for example, blue text can be displayed upon a yellow background, or the
green UK weather map can appear on a blue sea.

Boxed operation

This is one of a number of special features which increase the
versatility and effectiveness of Teletext. On suitable decoders
this allows a box of information to be inserted into the bottom of
a normal television picture. This, for example, would allow the
latest news flash to be displayed along with a normal picture. In
conjunction with suitable subtitles this system can be used to give
deaf people more pleasure from television than previously
possible.

Decoders often have a key called 'update' by which a new,
changed, page will be displayed. This enables a decoder to be set
to display a box of, say, a news flash in a normal television
programme when new news is transmitted. Once the viewer has
read the information, the use of the 'update' key would remove
it until further new information was transmitted. Once again,
special page header codes inform the decoder of the changes.

Double height display

This can be used with considerable effect on page headers, titles,
etc., and employs code bits to increase the character size to
twenty scan lines, instead of the usual ten. Forty characters per
row are still allowable with these double-sized alphanumerics as
they are only taller, not wider.

Flashing symbol and concealed display

These two features have not, as yet, seen much serious use. The former is self-explanatory, in that it allows any character to flash on and off – useful for calling it to the viewer's attention. The latter feature is more interesting, as it allows rows of text to be

Figure 6.16(a). Simple Teletext graphics, with the use of the 'reveal' function (Closed Circuit Consultants)

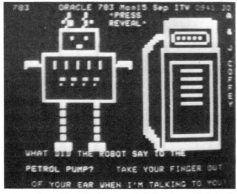

Figure 6.16(b). Having pressed the 'reveal' key the answer is displayed (Closed Circuit Consultants)

concealed until the 'reveal' key on the decoder is pressed. Thus a
quiz or test can be transmitted, with the answers being revealed
immediately on request (see *Figure 6.16*).

Time-coded pages

The page header contains a section where a time-of-day code can
be inserted, to allow a specific page to be displayed only when its
time-of-day code matches that selected by the viewer. This
allows very selective information retrieval. For example, a
rotating page set, all on page 150, might consist of weather
reports for Western Europe, with each capital city having a page
of its own. Without time codes each page might be transmitted
for five minutes and then replaced by the next, and so on. So to
see the third weather report in the batch, a viewer would have to
watch them all through. With time codes it can be arranged that
the set started on the hour, say at 11 o'clock and changed at
five-minute intervals. Thus setting the decoder time-code selector to page 150, 15 minutes, (that is, the third page of information) will ensure that only the required data are displayed.

   This feature has not been much used, although some commercial decoders allow its use as an 'alarm clock' for interrupting
normal television programmes by switching to Teletext at the
time selected by the viewer.

Telesoftware

This is an interesting development, designed to extend the use
and facilities of Teletext. Instead of normal pages of text, pages
of computer programs are transmitted. Special page headers tell
the decoder what these pages are, and also tell an associated
microprocessor, not found in conventional decoders, to store the
following page in the microprocessor memory, as opposed to
normal page store. The computer program can then be retrieved
and run on the microprocessor as convenient to the user. Typical
examples would include programs to calculate mortgage repay-
ments, diagnose simple illnesses, work out tax returns, do VAT
accounts, etc.

Teletext origination

Iaving seen how viewers can receive Teletext at home, let us
now examine how the broadcasters produce the information.

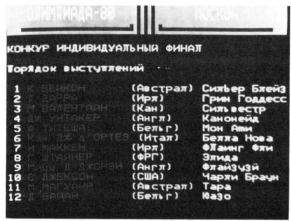

*Figure 6.17. An experimental BBC Teletext system for the Russian
Cyrillic alphabet, designed for the 1980 Olympic games (BBC)*

*Figure 6.18. The Ceefax newsroom where all the pages are
assembled and transmitted (BBC)*

(*Figures 6.17 and 6.18*). Although the ITV and BBC services are technically identical, they are organised in different ways. First of all, the general principles involved will be discussed.

Computers

The pages of information are assembled on VDUs (visual display units) from typewriter-like keyboards and the finished page can be checked and altered before being stored in the computer. Once the pages have been passed as being correct, they can be retrieved from the computer system at any time either for insertion into the television signals or for revision (news headlines, etc.).

Interface

The pages of Teletext information are broken down by the computer into their serially-coded bits and injected onto the required television lines (17, 330, 18, 331) automatically. Once a page has been transmitted in this manner, the next page is transmitted, and so on. *Figure 6.19* shows a block diagram of a typical Teletext computer system.

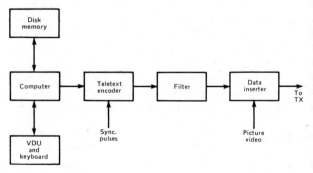

Figure 6.19. Basic Teletext computer system

Data bridges

Early on in the development of Teletext, the IBA (Independent Broadcasting Authority) ran into an interesting problem concerning the transmission of Teletext in various regions. As the information is generated in London and distributed with the networked programmes, it was realised that when a regional optout occurred, no Teletext could be transmitted, even though

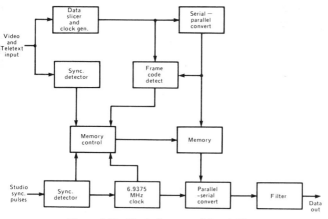

Figure 6.20. Block diagram of data bridge

a Thames or London Weekend Television standby feed was available in the studio. Anglia Television in Norwich built the first data bridge, a device which stripped the Teletext data from the incoming standby feed and inserted it into the outgoing local studio material. These devices have now become standard throughout the IBA network. *Figure 6.20* shows a block diagram of a typical data bridge. A local memory is required as the local and remote video sources are not necessarily in synchrony.

Viewdata

Having looked at Teletext, the UK broadcast version of videotext, let us now look at viewdata systems, as the non-

broadcast systems are known. In the UK the Post Office have
developed Prestel, a system for linking a domestic television set
with a remote computer by telephone line. Fortunately, as this
development occurred at about the same time as Teletext, a
broadly compatible joint specification was arrived at. This means
that many of the general principles outlined previously hold true
for both systems. Viewdata is a topic worthy of a complete book
to itself, but here space permits only an overview of the system.
Viewdata systems can be run in a number of ways, either on an
in-house basis for large firms with their own computers, or on a
public basis for the general business and domestic market.
Prestel is the Post Office (now British Telecom) viewdata system
of the latter type.

As viewdata systems have a direct line between a computer
and the user, they can be said to be truly interactive. Unlike
Teletext, viewdata pages are only transmitted to a specific user
at his request. As a telephone line is used, response time is
almost instantaneous. Another difference is that due to the
architecture of the data store, an almost unlimited database is
possible without sacrificing response time. At present the system

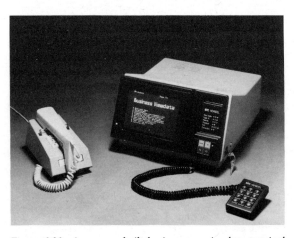

*Figure 6.21. A purpose-built business-use viewdata terminal
from STC (STC)*

is still under development, but computer centres are being built throughout the United Kingdom, and the Post Office hope that by 1984 over 90 per cent of telephone subscribers will have access to a Prestel computer via a local telephone call.

Another major difference between Prestel and Teletext is the cost involved. In both cases the viewer has to rent or purchase a modified television, or an add-on decoder unit, but after that Teletext is, at present, free, where as Prestel most decidedly is not! A typical Prestel charge is made up of three elements: the local phone call required to link the subscriber to the computer,

Figure 6.22. 14-inch colour viewdata terminal, for home or business use (Sony)

a computer time charge, related to the amount of computer time he uses, and a page charge. This latter cost is due to the fact that although the Post Office run Prestel, they do not provide the stored information. This is done by independent companies called Information Providers (IPs). Thus a page of up-to-date share information provided by a company may cost 50p to access with most of the 50p going to the company. Page prices vary between 0p and 50p, with most being around 3p. Although these costs may seem high, it should be remembered the Prestel is aimed at the business user as well as the domestic market.

Technical aspects

As Prestel is mainly compatible with Teletext, similar codes for characters, graphics, etc., are employed. *Figure 6.23* shows the Prestel code table which has a few differences from the Teletext one (*Figure 6.11*). In terms of transmission of information an asynchronous start/stop system is employed with a ten-bit code, compared with the Teletext seven-bit code. This consists of a start bit, seven data bits, a parity code and a stop bit. The data are modulated onto an audio tone to be transmitted down the telephone line at a rate of 1200 bits/second (120 characters per

B7				0	0	0	0	1	1	1	1
B6				0	0	1	1	0	0	1	1
B5				0	1	0	1	0	1	0	1
B4 B3 B2 B1	Col Row	0	1	2 / 2a	3 / 3a	4	4a	5	5a	6 / 6a	7 / 7a
0 0 0 0	0	NUL		Sp	0	@	NUL	P	DLE	—	p
0 0 0 1	1		DC1	!	1	A	ALPHA RED	Q	GRAPHICS RED	a	q
0 0 1 0	2		DC2	"	2	B	ALPHA GREEN	R	GRAPHICS GREEN	b	r
0 0 1 1	3		DC3	£	3	C	ALPHA YELLOW	S	GRAPHICS YELLOW	c	s
0 1 0 0	4		DC4	$	4	D	ALPHA BLUE	T	GRAPHICS BLUE	d	t
0 1 0 1	5	ENQ		%	5	E	ALPHA MAGENTA	U	GRAPHICS MAGENTA	e	u
0 1 1 0	6			&	6	F	ALPHA CYAN	V	GRAPHICS CYAN	f	v
0 1 1 1	7			'	7	G	ALPHA WHITE	W	GRAPHICS WHITE	g	w
1 0 0 0	8	BS	CANCEL	(	8	H	FLASH	X	CONCEAL	h	x
1 0 0 1	9	HT		)	9	I	STEADY	Y	CONTIGUOUS GRAPHICS	i	y
1 0 1 0	10	LF		*	:	J	END BOX	Z	SEPARATED GRAPHICS	j	z
1 0 1 1	11	VT	ESC	+	;	K	START BOX	←		k	¼
1 1 0 0	12	FF		,	<	L	NORMAL HEIGHT	½	BLACK BACKGROUND	l	‖
1 1 0 1	13	CR		—	=	M	DOUBLE HEIGHT	→	NEW BACKGROUND	m	¾
1 1 1 0	14		CURSOR HOME	.	>	N		↑	HOLD GRAPHICS	n	÷
1 1 1 1	15			/	?	O			RELEASE GRAPHICS	o	

COLUMNS 2a,3a,6a,7a produced after Graphics select code
COLUMNS 4a,5a produced after ESC code

Figure 6.23. Complete viewdata code table

second). This means that a complete page takes no longer than eight seconds to build up, compared with 23 seconds or so for Teletext, and in practice it only takes two or three seconds. The response rate from the user to the computer is much slower, being 75 bits/second (7½ characters per second). This is quite adequate as it is much faster than the user can press the keys.

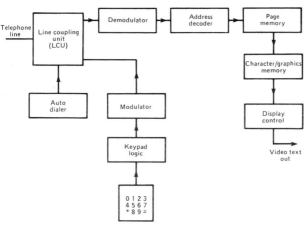

Figure 6.24. Prestel decoder block diagram

Figure 6.24 shows the block diagram of a typical Prestel decoder which can be compared with *Figure 6.8* which shows the comparable layout of the Teletext decoder. It will be noticed that in viewdata a user not only has the 0-9 keys, but also * and # as well. These keys allow the user to access any specific page, for example, by keying *123#. If *# is keyed, the previously selected page is retransmitted. If ** is used the currently selected page is retransmitted. This can be useful if any transmission errors have occurred.

Using Prestel

As an illustration of some of the features of Prestel, here is a description of a typical user session.

A viewer with a suitable decoder will either manually dial the local Prestel computer or, more likely, use a set with an auto-dialler in it. When the computer answers a 1.3 kHz tone is transmitted to the decoder, which then switches (either manually or automatically) into 'data', and automatically informs the computer that it is ready to accept data. The machine now responds by requesting the user's password, which prevents unauthorised access to the system as each user has a unique password. (*Figure 6.25*). Once this has been accepted a 'welcome' page is transmitted, which by keying will be replaced by page 0, the general index. It is here that the novel indexing system used by Prestel comes into its own. Page 0 lists nine separate choices (*Figure 6.26*) of further types of information. By selecting 5 the viewer will go to Business Prestel. This page (5) has nine further choices which can be selected. If 8 is

Figure 6.25. A Prestel terminal in use in a domestic situation. Note the simple hand-held remote control pad (British Telecom)

Figure 6.26. The Prestel information tree (Mullard)

requested, page 58 will be displayed. This has only three choices. Number 2 will take the viewer to page 582 and so it is not necessary to go through all the pages if it is known that page 582455 is the desired one. This can be addressed directly by keying *582455# from page 0. This can help reduce the cost involved by cutting out unnecessary pages and by reducing

Figure 6.27. A typical page from Prestel (Closed Circuit Consultants)

phone call time. Before the user switches off, he can request an update on his Prestel bill. Incidentally, if a page selection is chargeable, the cost is always shown on the currently-selected page. This ensures that the user knows how much a page will cost before he accesses it, thus giving him the choice of not going to it because it is too expensive (*Figure 6.27*).

Direct response frames

As Prestel is a two-way communications medium it allows direct interaction between user and computer. In some experimental instances this has been put to an educational end, such as

ꞓrogrammed learning, computer-assisted learning, computer-
ꞓnstructed learning, etc. In other cases more commercial uses
ꞓave been developed, such as direct mail order via Prestel. It
ꞓorks like this. A firm, a bookseller for example, lists the
ꞓurrent top ten books, along with a review of each one on a set of
ꞓrestel pages. A special response page allows a viewer (even
ꞓith a basic *# 0 – 9 keyboard) to select, say, book number 7
ꞓnd purchase it. The computer then sends his order, along with
ꞓis name and address (which has been retrieved from the

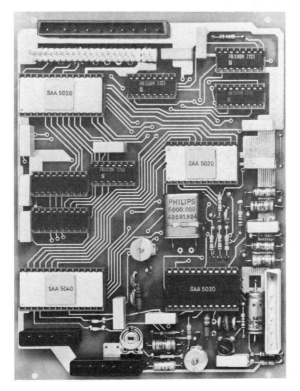

*Figure 6.28. A typical 'state-of-the-art' teletext/viewdata
decoder (Mullard)*

computer's user-records) to the firm's Prestel terminal, who then posts the customer the required book and invoices him.

This service is already run by various travel firms, wine shops etc. Obviously special checks are needed to ensure that the customer really gets what he wants and that only the authorised user can order from the terminal. The system can even be linked to credit card numbers to avoid extra paper work. Personally although I find it an interesting idea, I find my will power weakens considerably when I access the wine merchant's page!

Hardware

Numerous manufacturers make add-on decoders for Prestel or complete television sets. (*Figure 6.28*). Often the latter are suitable for the reception of both Prestel and Teletext. Some manufacturers also make purpose-built business terminals which cannot be used as off-air television sets or Teletext receivers. *Figure 6.29* shows a block diagram of a dual purpose Teletext/ Viewdata receiver from Mullard. Although the cost of purchasing a Prestel set outright is rather high at present (£600

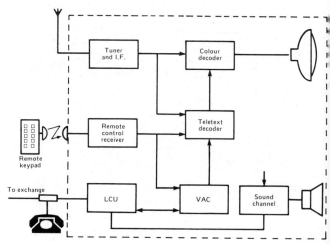

Figure 6.29. Mullard Prestel/Teletext decoder block diagram

upwards) prices are coming down, and will continue to do so as demand and mass-production increases. Running costs are obviously going to depend on usage, but will not be insubstantial.

Information providers

The 0 – 9*# keyboard is adequate for domestic use, but does not allow information to be put into the system. For this an alphanumeric keyboard, with editing controls is required (*Figure*

Figure 6.30. A full alphanumeric viewdata keyboard (Sony)

6.30). Information providers pay the Post Office for being allowed to put pages into the system and recoup their costs from the charges made to the users for page access.

Developments

With several decoders it is already possible to off-load pages of information onto ordinary audio cassettes for replaying at a later

date. This might allow non-topical information to be maintained
at a local library, although the copyright aspect of this is far from
clear.

Another development is that of an add-on printer for making
hard copies of pages (*Figure 6.31*). Black and white ones are

*Figure 6.31. Hard copy of any videotext can be obtained by the
used of a suitable printer (Sony)*

already available, and full colour ones have been demonstrated.
The compatibility between viewdata and Teletext ensures that
these types of accessories can be used with either system.

Full colour high-definition still pictures

This is one of the most recent additions to the facilities offered
by Prestel, and when fully implemented will allow an information provider to mix high-quality full-colour stills with text on the
same page. This would allow, for example, estate agents to show
pictures of properties for sale as well as describing them, as they
do at present. Other uses would cover advertising, product sales,
signature verification, etc.

Picture Prestel, which can also be applied to broadcasting Teletext, employs a modified decoder in the receiver to enable it to receive and decode the picture information. This information is provided by digitally dissecting a colour photograph and encoding it as Differential Pulse Code Modulation (DPCM). The coded signal is then transmitted in the normal way and stored in a large memory (25 K bits) in the receiver. A microprocessor and control circuit then display the full-colour still on the screen. The building-up process takes around 60 seconds, which is rather long. Experimental techniques, at

Figure 6.32. A public access viewdata terminal which can be used with 10p and 50p coins (ISE)

present under development, could reduce this to around 1-15 seconds. Picture size is also at present limited to around one-third of the available screen size, but again it is highly possible that this can be improved upon.

Coin-operated Prestel

Although Prestel was originally developed for domestic and business use a demand for it in public places, such as hotels and railway stations, has become apparent. To cope with this special coin-operated terminals have been developed which accept 10p and 50p coins and have a degree of local intelligence. That is, instructions are displayed on the screen to guide a user through the steps required to operate the terminal. (*Figure 6.32*). This is essential to enable the inexpert viewer to get optimum results from the system. When not in use the television screen can be used to display various advertisements, etc.

Foreign systems

Although both Teletext and Viewdata are British-designed systems, many overseas firms have been demonstrating an interest in this field.

France

After the British, it is the French who have the second largest stake in the videotext market. Although they are not as yet operating a nation-wide service by either broadcast television or telephone lines, various local services are fully operational. Developed jointly by the PTT and TDF (National Television), Antiope (Acquisition Numérique et Télévisualisation d'Images Organisées en Pages d'Écriture) is a Teletext system broadcast

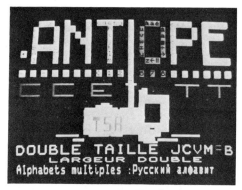

Figure 6.33. Antiope, the French teletext system (French PTT)

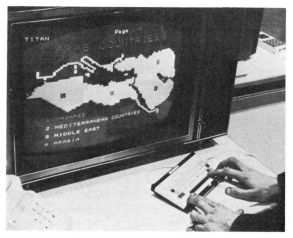

Figure 6.34. Titan, the interactive French viewdata system (French PTT)

on spare television lines as in UK. (*Figure 6.33*). It also has the capabilities of occupying a complete television channel for out-of-hours high-speed data transfer. It is completely compatible with Titan, the French telephone viewdata system which is being tested in 3000 houses in Velizy, a Paris suburb (*Figure 6.34*).

Canada

Telidon, the Canadian Teletext/viewdata system was developed during the late 1970s and has a high-resolution graphics capability as one of its major features. (*Figure 6.35*). It can provide around 320×280 picture elements resolution as opposed to around 60×80 for British Teletext. The use of a microprocessor-based decoder allows for this high resolution but it also raises the

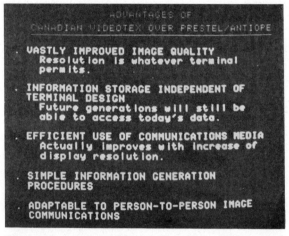

Figure 6.35. Canadian Telidon is said to offer various advantages over the UK system (Canadian Department of Communications)

cost of the decoder to the viewer. At present no full commercial service has been inaugurated, though field trials are being conducted. Over £12 million has been invested by the Canadian Government, so the subject is being taken quite seriously. It seems probable that what ever service is implemented in the USA will be also adopted by the Canadians. Bell Canada have a

1000-terminal system called Vista under trial at present (1980) in the Toronto area. Although capable of using the Telidon format, this trial system can also use the UK Prestel format.

USA

Somewhat surprisingly, the USA was not, and is still not, a leader in the videotext field. A number of user-trials have been conducted, probably the first being a single-line subtitle service for the deaf conducted by the Public Broadcasting Service in Washington, DC. This used line 21 for data carrying and was started in 1977, but is now being discontinued as it has been overtaken by other developments. Other trials of British Ceefax and French Antiope have been conducted as well as those of some American systems such as Micro Television's Infotext and Reuter's 'News Views'.

Japan

The Japanese have a considerable problem when it comes to text by television systems as their alphabet consists of over 2000 pictographs, as compared with the 26 letters in English. However, CIBS (Character Information Broadcasting Station) a NHK (Nippon Hoso Kyokai – National Television Company) development was proposed in February 1976 and implemented in Autumn 1978 as an experimental service providing subtitles for the deaf, weather forecasts, etc. (*Figure 6.36*). Like UK Teletext, it employs the spare television lines in the frame blanking period, but it also needs a large amount of memory in the decoder, thus increasing the cost to the user. The pictographs are built up by matrices with 332 dots per line, and 200 lines per page. The Japanese PTT has developed Captains (Character And Pattern Telephone Access Information Network System) which is similar to UK Prestel. A field trial of 1000 houses is at present being conducted. Various other experimental systems are being investigated, including Asahi's Telescan in Osaka which superimposes a data display as a crawling strip on a normal television picture. This is somewhat similar to the news headline's displays sometimes seen in public places, where a strip

Figure 6.36. Nippon TV's CIBS teletext system, capable of producing high-resolution graphics (NHK)

of a single line of characters slowly crawls from right to left across a screen.

West Germany

From 1979 onwards, a number of field trials of modified UK Prestel and Teletext systems were conducted culminating in a 2000 user trial in the Düsseldorf/Neuss area of the viewdata system in 1980.

Other Countries

Holland and all the Scandinavian countries have experimented with variations on the UK systems, although only Sweden and Denmark have operational systems, the latter having been started in 1977. Hong Kong has purchased the United Kingdom Teletext system and Teletext trials have been conducted in Australia. Belgium, Switzerland, Colombia and Singapore are a few of the other nations actively involved in videotext development with either public or experimental services.

Videotext – the future

It seems probable, in the UK at least, that combined Prestel/ Teletext television terminals will fall in price and thus become more widespread. That industry will produce Prestel-only units for commercial use is already a reality. This market will probably increase in size – hopefully subsidising the development costs for the domestic user's equipment. The use of Prestel for electronic mail – that is, leaving messages for other subscribers – will become more commonplace and begin to attack the Telex market, particularly in the small business/domestic end. Whatever happens, videotext is here to stay.

7 Video games

While VTRs and colour cameras are owned by only a very small percentage of the population, this cannot be said for television games. Even those people who do not own a TV game have probably seen or played with one in a pub, club or even a motorway service station! From January to July 1980, inclusive, 356,994 TV games, worth £3,933,000 were imported into the UK.

The first TV games to appear in the UK in 1972, were of the black and white ping-pong type and designed for amusement arcade use. Shortly after this, similar games became available for domestic use, but these were expensive and relied upon a large number of integrated circuits – a spin-off from computer electronics. It was the introduction in 1975 of a ping-pong type integrated circuit by General Instruments that paved the way for the highly sophisticated TV games we are familiar with today. The use of this integrated circuit reduced the parts count of a typical game from around 150 to about 15, and allowed a corresponding reduction in price. Following on from simple football, tennis and ping-pong, more complex games began to appear, including those such as motor racing which had primitive graphics of cars moving around an oval race track. The addition of colour, as demonstrated by the British firm of Sportel in 1977 increased the interest in TV games. It soon became apparent that something more complex than tennis or football was required to maintain a viewer's interest in the game, and two alternative solutions were developed.

The first of these relied on the production of custom-designed integrated circuits to allow a complete circuit to be based around a specific game, sometimes with some variations. Examples of this type include tank warfare, a motor bike scramble and a space invader game. Again though, from the manufacturer's point of view, the design and production costs of this type of game are quite high, and can only be justified if massive sales are anticipated.

The second approach is to sell the consumer a basic TV game unit, containing most of the expensive components, (power supply, UHF modulator, games controls, etc.) and allow him to purchase, as required, additional 'plug-in' cartridges which allow a variety of games to be played. These plug-in games also fall into two categories, semi-programmable and fully-programmable.

Semi-programmable games

The introduction of these games allowed, for the first time, a user to play a wide range of games, by purchasing additional plug-in cartridges. In practice, each of these contained an integrated circuit which was a complete game; the main case contained a power supply, UHF modulator and all the other electronics needed for any TV game. The problem with this type of game is that, as each cartridge contains a custom-built integrated circuit, the development costs, and hence the sale price, are relatively high.

Programmable games

These represent the latest generation of TV games, and cater for an almost unlimited repertoire of games. Like the semi-programmable machines, these consist of a basic unit into which game cartridges can be plugged. However, unlike semi-programmable games, the cartridges contain only a ROM (read-only memory), a semiconductor device which stores a computer program (for further details of this and other video terms see the Glossary). The base unit contains a microprocessor which converts these instructions into a display on a TV screen. The great advantage of this type of game is that although the costs of the main base unit may be slightly higher than for semi-programmable games, the cost of cartridges is lower and the range almost infinite. Different games are produced by loading different instructions into the memory cartridge, a relatively cheap operation, and one which can be done economically even when only low sales are anticipated. Programmable games also score over other types by using components which are all off-the-shelf stock items, unlike dedicated games where special, expensive, integrated circuits are needed.

How the TV game interfaces with the TV set, some examples of the various types and the technical aspects of TV game operation will be dealt with next.

Connections

All the games discussed are of the type that plugs into the aerial socket of a normal TV set. This means that the signal from the games unit to the TV has to appear to the TV to be a normal aerial signal. This is achieved by converting the output from the games integrated circuit into a UHF radio frequency signal by means of a modulator. This device is effectively a miniature TV transmitter and is the same as that found in VTRs. It combines a sound and a vision signal into a UHF signal, usually around channel 36. This can be selected on the TV and a spare tuner button allocated to it if desired. If considerable use is made of a TV game, a small switch box can be purchased into which both TV aerial and TV games are plugged. The switch output is fed to the TV and a switch used to select either TV game or off-air television. This obviates the problem of continually removing and replacing aerial plugs, which are not particularly robust. Most TV games are operated from 12 V d.c. often supplied by a mains power unit, although some units use dry cell batteries. With heavy use this can become rather expensive.

Dedicated bat and ball games

The very first of these were built-up from separate integrated circuits, were physically quite large and used a lot of power. Although a few of this type did appear on the domestic market (more so in the USA), they found their main homes in pubs and amusement arcades. The well known 'Pong' game was of this type. UK enthusiasts were given the opportunity to build their own TV game by following a series of articles published in the magazine 'Television' in 1974. Using computer-type integrated circuits, even at 1974 prices, the basic table-tennis game cost around £70 to build!

The first dedicated bat and ball game based around a single integrated circuit was introduced the following year and was based on the General Instruments AY–3–8500 chip. This formed the basis for a number of games, including football, tennis, squash and a rifle-shooting game, which relied on an optional plug-in 'rifle' consisting of a photo-cell that was aimed at a moving target (a bright square) on the screen. Not only did this chip reduce the cost of TV games, but with its on-screen scoring and basic sound effects it increased their entertainment value. Technically, the chip is quite a large one, having 28 pins, but it needs only two dozen additional components to form a complete black and white game.

From the electronic point of view, although there is a wide variation between different types of games from different manu-facturers, they all have certain features in common. In a simple black and white game of the 'pong' type, using the AY–3–8500 chip, the two players' controls feed signals to a block of game-control logic circuitry, which in turn controls the display generation logic. The appearance of a ball in this type of game is achieved by selectively delaying the line and field synchronising

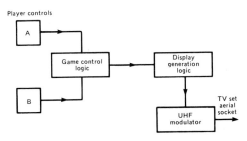

Figure 7.1. Basic TV game block diagram

signals, inverting them, and where they intersect, using them to produce a block of display. The delay is proportional to the movement of the hand controllers. The very simplest type of hand controller is the 'paddle', which is in fact a single sliding potentiometer; move it up or down and the bat moves up or down. Joystick controls are needed to allow both up and down, as well as left to right, motion and are found on some of the more complex games. This type of graphics display is rather limited and a different technique is used in the microprocessor-type games.

National Semiconductors chose 1977 as the year in which to release their rival integrated circuit, which was capable of generating a colour picture. As well as the games chip, this

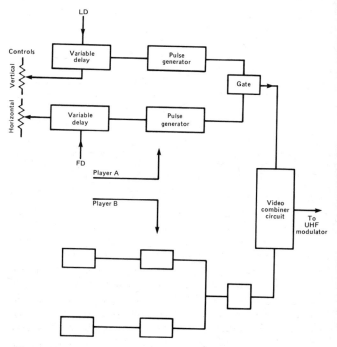

Figure 7.2. Detailed block diagram of simple TV game logic circuits

approach needed two integrated circuits and about two dozen additional components. One of these integrated circuits was a highly accurate oscillator, while the other acted not only as a colour coder but also as an RF modulator. The unit was of the 'pong' type, catering for tennis, squash, football, etc.

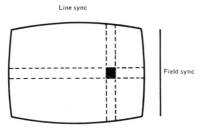

Line sync

Field sync

Figure 7.3. Representation of 'player' on simple TV game screen showing relationship to line and field syncs

Various other manufacturers marketed games units based on these chip sets and even in 1980 one can still buy a basic colour six-game 'pong' unit for under £10. A similar ten-game unit, offering hockey, basketball, solo basketball. solo squash, football, gridball, tennis, squash and two target games, in colour, with switchable bat size and fast or slow speed is available from Ingersoll as the XK 410C, at about £30.

Semi-programmable games

A typical semi-programmable game would be the Ingersoll XK 4000 'Strike Command' which has about ten cartridges available for it. The base unit contains the power unit, game selector switches, player control and much of the electronics. The plug-in cartridge houses the actual game, integrated circuit and a few other components. Typical of this type of game are those built around the General Instruments chip set, which also includes the Waddington Videomaster colour cartridge, Binatone Superstar and the Teleplay game. Electrically, all these are almost identical although the stylings and prices vary. Although the plug-in cartridges for any one game, say Tank Battle, all contain identical components, those supplied by one manufacturer will not fit the base unit of another manufacturer.

The base units all have two hand controllers, with joysticks and 12 or 14 push button keys. The functions of these vary depending on the game being played. A further four switches are on the base unit itself and control game start, reset, on/off and select game. This latter feature allows any one of up to twelve games contained in each cartridge to be selected. A 32-pole multi-way socket accommodates the matching cartridge,

About 14 or 15 cartridges are available and these cater for a wide range of tastes. All are colour-capable, with added sound effects, although the graphics are not quite as good as those produced by the more sophisticated and expensive fully-programmable games.

Most of the dedicated chips (ICs) are of the General Instruments AY–3–8 xxx ranges, which, at present, covers the following types. Different manufacturers call their versions by different names, but their ancestry is fairly obvious:

AY–3–8710 Tank Battle
AY–3–8765 Stunt Rider
AY–3–8603 Road Racer
AY–3–8610 10 Games (Pong)
AY–3–8605 Spacewar
AY–3–8606 Breakout
AY–3–8760 Stunt Cycle
AY–3–8600 10 Games (Pong)

Fully-programmable games

With these we move into the world of microprocessors, and the dividing line between small computers such as Apple and Pet and games like the Philips G7000 and the Atari becomes very hazy indeed.

The programmable games all contain a microprocessor and the plug-in cartridges a ROM (*Figure 7.4*). The possibilities of such a system are almost limitless and although the costs of the base unit are initially high, the cost of the plug-in modules is low. This is because they contain a standard computer type chip, rather than a specially designed games chip. The ROMs are programmed with computer instructions for each game during manufacture by a system called mask programming. This means that they can be mass-produced at a low cost.

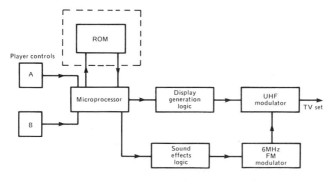

Figure 7.4. Programmable TV game block diagram

One of the first true programmable games was the Video Master 'Database' which is built around the Mullard (Signetics) microprocessor chip set. Each games cartridge contains 8×2 K byte ROMs which hold the programme instructions for the various games. Using the same chip set are also the Acetronic MPU 1000, Prinztronic VC 6000, Radofin 1292–1392, Audiosonic PP 1292, Hanimex HMG 1292 and the Teleng 'Colourstars' game. Electrically these are almost identical, although only memory cartridges from Prinztronic, Radofin and Acetronic are physically interchangeable. Although designed to foster brand loyalty, in the long term this seems to be working against these games, as customers become frustrated by the lack of availability of specific games. A similar problem also arose with the General Instruments dedicated games chip semi-programmable games, such as Teleplay. About 14 or 16 games are available for the Signetics-based system, covering a wide range of interests.

Cartridge 1 contains a number of 'pong' type games and as such is not very exciting. Tank and aeroplane combat is covered by cartridge number 2, while number 3 is a horse racing game. A maze comes in number 4, and 5 and 6 are designed to develop a child's maths ability. Simple problems are set and the viewer can key in a suitable answer. A variant of noughts and crosses called 'four in a row' comes in cartridge number 7, and a variant of the 'Mastermind' peg and board game is in number 8. More air and sea battles can be played with number 9 while more personal combat in the form of boxing comes with number 10 cartridge. The remaining games are blackjack, clay-pigeon shoot, motor sport and circus – this last being a skill game including jumping acrobats, etc.

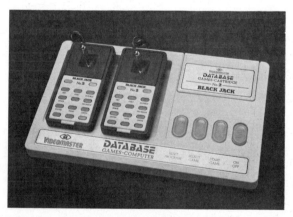

Figure 7.5. Database programmable game, with plug-in cartridges (Waddingtons)

This type of system has considerable scope for expansion as further games can be manufactured and plugged-in. From the customer's point of view the base unit costs around £90 and the cartridges about £15.

Following on from these early fully-programmable games come the latest models, such as the Atari and Mattel games, which are again microprocessor-based, but offer even more features. The Atari is based on the Signetics 2650 microprocessor chip, and the plug-in cartridges contain ROMs. Most of the electronics are housed in the main case, which also has game select, difficulty and reset switching. The cartridges plug in a slot in the top and three types of controllers are available, a simple keyboard, a joystick and a 'paddle' type. Full colour graphics, with sound effects are possible and about three dozen cartridges are at present available, some housing up to 112 different games. Besides the games mentioned previously in this section, some novel games are available, including Space Invaders, chess, Superman and bowling. Some games have an educational slant, such as basic maths, braingame and hangman (*Figure 7.6*).

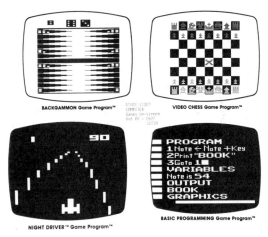

BACKGAMMON Game Program™

ATARI VIDEO
COMPUTER
Games on-screen
RNA PR - 0620
3Z0139

VIDEO CHESS Game Program™

NIGHT DRIVER™ Game Program™

BASIC PROGRAMMING Game Program™

Figure 7.6. Off-screen visuals of a number of Atari TV games
(Atari)

The Mattel Intellivision must be one of the most sophisticated games on the market today, as its price of around £200 and £19 each for the cartridges would suggest. A 16-bit microprocessor is used, as opposed to the eight-bit ones employed in most other programmable games, and this allows for a more ambitious approach. Besides the normal colour graphics and sound effects, a very realistic 3D display is also possible. This is achieved by, amongst other things, not using the normal low-resolution graphics building-block approach, but by borrowing a technique from the computer world called 'memory mapping'. As well as a simple keyboard and combined paddle control, a full computer keyboard is also available, with a built-in cassette deck and 16 K of memory storage. This allows the Mattel to be used as a fully-fledged domestic computer system. As mentioned previously, the dividing line between TV games and computers is very tenuous! The games available fall into three groups; sports (football, etc.), thinking (chess) and educational (maths).

Another interesting programmable game is the Philips G7000 Videopac. When first introduced in late 1978, this game showed great promise, as it incorporated a full alphanumeric QWERTY touch-sensitive keyboard. This allowed the possibility of a user writing his own computer program, as well as playing a number of interesting and well-designed games. Unfortunately Philips chose to use a complex hexadecimal language for their microprocessor instead of the more familiar and easier BASIC. This tended to reduce its appeal.

Two further devices which fall into the category of TV games are video synthesisers and a unique product from Videomaster called 'Star Chess'.

Video synthesisers

Over recent years a number of units which produce various moving coloured patterns on the TV screen have been marketed, with varying degrees of success (*Figure 7.7*). Generally speaking, these units produce a simple pattern, say two vertical bars, the colour, position and thickness of which is modulated, often in response to an external audio signal. When used in conjunction with a hi-fi, this type of TV add-on can produce an interesting effect. More sophisticated units are available which produce more complex patterns including squares, ovals, etc. The input from a black and white TV camera can also be colourised in this way. When used in discotheques, either on TV projection equipment or banks of monitors, they can be very impressive but

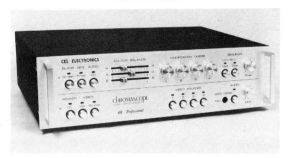

Figure 7.7. A new product, which generates coloured patterns on a TV screen in time to music (CEL)

in a domestic situation their use is limited. In the USA Atari produce a 'Videomusic' cartridge for their TV games which produces this type of effect.

'Star Chess'

This unique product is two-person television game, which produces a chessboard-like dispay on a TV screen. By using hand controllers the two players can manipulate their pieces around

Figure 7.8. The Atari 400 and 800 domestic computers can also be used to play games (Atari)

the board according to various rules. Unlike conventional chess, however, the pieces are named after various space craft and do not obey the normal chess rules. For example, it is possible for a piece to 'dematerialise' off the board and to reappear at a random location later in the game. Although 'Star Chess' is fascinating to play, it should be remembered that it is a dedicated non-programmable game and that it cannot be used to play

Figure 7.9. Atari also produce a sophisticated microprocessor-controlled TV game, with a wide range of cartridges (Atari)

normal chess. With this in mind, as well as its £40 price tag, its appeal is limited and it is being overtaken by the various programmable games.

It seems reasonable to expect the market to crystallise into three areas. The first and cheapest (around £10) for which demand will decrease, will be the basic non-programmable game suitable for young children. This will be followed by the more expensive (around £50 – £100), programmable game which will be the major part of the market. It is expected that the number of games will increase and that independent software houses will start to market cartridges for sale to owners of brand-leader games.

The final section of the market and the most expensive, (around £400), will be true domestic computers, which when not being used for their true business or educational purposes, can be used to play games. These usually rely on computer floppy discs or cassette tapes as a means of storing program instructions, although the Atari 400 and 800 can use either.

Glossary of terms and abbreviations

AC (a.c.) Alternating current, as supplied by the mains.

Address Term used for memory location in computer systems.

AFC Automatic frequency control.

AGC Automatic gain control.

AM Amplitude modulation; the variation in intensity of a signal of fixed carrier frequency.

Amplitude Level or intensity of a signal.

Antiope French video text system.

Azimuth Angle between a magnetic recording/relay head and the plane of the head-to-tape motion.

Bandwidth Part of frequency spectrum occupied by a signal.

Baud Number of bits per second, as used in defining the speed of digital systems.

Bit BInary digiT, the basic unit of digital information transfer.

Byte A number of bits which make up a digital instruction, as used in microprocessor systems.

Belling-Lee Trade name for a type of high frequency plug system, as fitted on TV aerials.

Beta Domestic video cassette system originated by Sony.

Bias High frequency signal applied to audio tape to reduce distortion; or control signal applied to semiconductor circuits.

Black level Darkest portion of a TV signal, below which there can be no picture information.

BNC Video plug and socket system, using a bayonet fitting.

Burn Retention of a black mark on a TV camera tube which has been exposed to a very bright light.

Captains Videotext system as used in Japan.

Carrier Electronic signal onto which other signals are modulated.

CED   Capacitive Electronic Disc, the current name for the RCA video disc system; originally called Selectavision.

Chromium dioxide   Oxide coating used on some recording tape which has a higher overloading point and better image-retention properties than ferric oxide tape.

Colour temperature   Measure of the colour quality of light; the higher the temperature, the more blue in it.

Composite video   A video signal which includes both picture and synchronising information.

Control track   Track on video tape used for recording servo information.

CPU   Central Processing Unit; the major functional unit of a microprocessor or computer system.

Crispener   Electronic device for enhancing the horizontal resolution of TV pictures.

CRT   Cathode Ray Tube, the display device in most TV sets.

Ceefax   BBC videotext service; from 'See Facts'.

DC (d.c.)   Direct current; a constant level of voltage or current.

DIN   West German equivalent of the British Standards Institute, one specification of which applies to various types of audio connectors.

Dolby   Dolby, Ray. American electronics engineer who was involved in the development of the quadruplex VTR, and more recently a tape noise reduction system used on both audio cassettes and some video machines.

Drop-out   Area of magnetic tape on which the oxide coating is damaged and hence no signal will be recorded.

Dubbing   (1) Adding sound to video, post production. (2) A method of duplicating U-matic format video tapes.

Edit   To join sections of video tape, usually electronically.

EIAJ   Electronic Industries Association of Japan, who developed a standardised half-inch open-reel video tape format.

Eidophor   Swiss large-screen projection TV system.

EPROM   Erasable Programmable Read-Only Memory, a semiconductor memory device.

Equalise   To alter the characteristics of a sound or vision signal in a controlled manner.

FM   Frequency Modulation; variation of the frequency of a carrier signal, while the amplitude remains constant.

Field   Half a TV frame. Two fields (odd and even) make a frame.

Gen-lock   Method of synchronising two or more video cameras to allow them to be mixed.

Guard band   The area of blank tape between video tracks on non-azimuth recording VTRs.

Hardware   The machinery of a computer as opposed to the programs and operating systems (software).

Head drum   Part of the VTR which houses the video heads.

Helical   A type of video format where the video tracks are recorded across the tape diagonally, as in helical scan.

HF   High frequency, normally applied to radio signals.

Hz   Hertz; the unit of frequency, one cycle per second.

Impedance   Measurement of a.c. resistance, as applied to the matching of input and output signals in video equipment.

Infra-red   High frequency light rays which are invisible to the human eye. Used in video remote control units.

Joystick   A bi-directional control used in TV games to give vertical and horizontal movement of the bat, etc.

'Laserdisc'   Trade name for a system using a laser to produce and replay video discs.

Laservision   Name of the Philips video disc system, once known as VLP (Video Long Play).

LCD   Liquid Crystal Display. Type of alphanumeric display coming into use for tape counters, timers etc.

LED   Light-Emitting Diode. Type of alphanumeric display used in some VTRs for counters, etc.

Line   One scanning line of a TV picture. In UK PAL, 625 lines make a complete picture. In the USA the corresponding figure is 525 lines.

Lumen   Measure of light level, from the sun or artifical lights.

Luminance   Often abbreviated as luma; the black and white part of a colour video signal.

Lux   Measure of light level.

Microprocessor   Semiconductor device which can be used for a wide range of tasks, depending on its programming.

Modulator   A device which turns a video signal into a TV signal.

Monitor   Type of TV which accepts video and audio level signals but has no TV tuner.

Monochrome   Often abbreviated to mono. Black and white.

NTSC   Colour system used in the USA; also as Modified NTSC, which has a colour subcarrier frequency of 4.43 MHz, thus making it possible to play back Modified NTSC tapes on some special PAL type equipment.

Oracle   Optical Reception of Announcements by Coded Line Electronics; videotext service run by the Independent TV companies.

PAL   Phase Alternative Line; UK colour TV system.

PCM   Pulse Code Modulation; digital signal encoding.

Prestel   Videotext system run by British Telecom.

Program   A series of instructions for a computer to follow.

Programme   Pre-recorded TV material.

PROM   Programmable Read-Only Memory; a type of semiconductor memory device.

Quadruplex   Broadcast standard VTR.

RAM   Random Access Memory; a semiconductor memory device

ROM   Read-Only Memory.

SECAM   French colour TV system

Selectavision   RCA's video disc system, now called CED.

Software   Computer programs and operating systems as opposed to the actual machinery (hardware).

Splice   To join together lengths of tape.

Standards converter   Device for turning PAL video signals into NTSC or SECAM, and vice versa.

Sync   Synchronising pulses, as in TV line and field pulses.

TeD   Teldec. Obsolete video disc system relying on a mechanical pickup.

Teletext   Videotext information system using normal television transmitters and spare lines of the TV signal.

Telesoftware   Computer programs distributed to domestic users by videotext systems.

Track   Information recorded on magnetic tape in the form of a band.

Tracking   A measure of the accuracy with which a video tape is replayed.

Trinitron   TV tube manufactured by Sony, employing in-line guns and colour stripes.

UHF (F and E) PL259   Type of video connector using a screw thread.

U-matic   Industrial video tape recorder developed by Sony and adopted by many other manufacturers as an industrial standard.

VCR   Philips trade name for their domestic video tape recorder; often used as an abbreviation for Video Cassette Recorder.

VCR-LP   Also a Philips trade name, for their long-playing domestic video tape recorder.

VHS   Video Home System; domestic video tape system developed by JVC of Japan.

Vertical interval   Blank space in the formation of a TV signal, often used for the transmission of videotext information.

Video cassette   Plastic container housing video tape.

VTR   Video tape recorder; a device for recording TV pictures on magnetic tape.

Video disc   Disc on which TV pictures are recorded.

Videogram   Pre-recorded TV programme available on video tape or video disc.

Video 2000   Trade name of Philips double-sided video cassette format.

Viewdata   Videotext system employing telephone land-lines.

Visc   Trade name for a now obsolete video disc system developed by Matsushita.

VLP   Video Long Play; obsolete trade name for Philips video disc system, now called Laservision.

Word   Unit of information, made up of binary digits, used in computer terminology.

Zoom lens   TV lens which can change its focal length while maintaining focus.

Index